Experience Required

How to become a UX leader regardless of your role

Robert Hoekman Jr

VOICES THAT MATTER™

Experience Required: How to become a UX leader regardless of your role
Robert Hoekman Jr

New Riders
www.newriders.com

To report errors, please send a note to errata@peachpit.com

New Riders is an imprint of Peachpit, a division of Pearson Education
Copyright © 2016 by Robert M. Hoekman

Senior Editor: Karyn Johnson
Development Editor: Robyn Thomas
Production Editor: David Van Ness
Copyeditor: Scout Festa
Proofreader: Liz Welch
Compositor: WolfsonDesign
Indexer: Rebecca Plunkett
Interior Design: Mimi Heft
Cover Design: Robert Hoekman Jr, Mimi Heft

ISBN-13: 978-0-134-39827-3
ISBN-10:   0-134-39827-0

9 8 7 6 5 4 3 2 1

Printed and bound in the United States of America

▶ Contents

Preface

▶ Who You Are and Why You're Reading This

You might be a director of UX. You might be a student learning how to join the legion of designers already out in the world. You might be a free-lancer offering your design-slinging services to small businesses in your city. You might be a member of a team deep inside a major company that has invented a hundred different web products with a separate team for each one. You're a consultant. You're a newbie. You're an intern. Your position is irrelevant. So is your title.

No matter your status or situation, you're in a position to lead, to raise the bar where it consistently sits lower than you think it should, to discover that the bar *needs* to be raised, and how to help make it happen.

Here's who you might be and how you might benefit from this book.

If You're a Designer

One of the most common questions to come out of a designer's mouth is "How do I stop being an afterthought and learn to lead UX efforts?" Sometimes the question comes from people who already *are* leading UX efforts.

You need to know how to get yourself into a concept meeting. You need to know how to convince people you're right. How to get your ideas moving forward. How to take charge. How to build the reputation that will enable stakeholders in your projects to give you their complete trust, and how to keep it. How to grow. How to keep yourself happy in the job so you don't spend your whole career wondering about the grass on the other side of the street. It's a lot. This book covers the skills you don't already have.

If You're a Student

You hope to get a low-level designer gig at a major company where you can learn at a relaxed pace, or go to work for some cool startup where you can learn from fast, smart designers who crank out cutting-edge products with weekly updates. What you need to know is not how to design well—you're drowning in that kind of knowledge already. What you need to know is how to demonstrate to people that you can contribute in a meaningful way. How and when to make your way into a more influential position. You need to know what you don't know. What they're not teaching you. This book shows you how to convince people of your recommendations, how to know they're good, when to learn, when to jump, and how to get the most out of your job choice.

If You're an Instructor

You teach design classes at a community college, an art institute, or a major university. Maybe you teach workshops to design teams within large companies or startups. Your biggest concern is knowing *what to teach*. So far, you've focused on hard skills: usability testing, interaction design, building a prototype with some cool new code framework. What employers and clients actually want is a designer who is flexible and right. This book shows you the essential soft skills that will make your students more effective from their first day, whether as an intern or a staffer.

If You're a Hiring Manager

One of the most common questions to come out of a startup owner's mouth when it comes to design is "How do I know who to hire?"

You might be a small business owner looking for the perfect freelance web designer to build you a quick, reasonably priced website for your shop or accounting business or something else. You might be an HR rep in a large company whose job it is to weed out the first round of candidates. Whatever your situation, you're tasked with finding, interviewing, and choosing the person or team that builds the products that define your company. Any addition to the team changes its energy, its focus, its abilities. You need to find the person with the right skills and qualities. This book shows you what great designers do and say and think so you can spot them in your interviews and help them do what they already want to do well.

If You're a Design Director

You've been a designer for a long time. You may have a solid handle on it. You may not. What you need to do now is help *other* people become better at it. You need to know the difference between managing and leading. You need to know how to make everyone else on the team better. You need to know why a small group is better than an individual, and why a *team*'s reputation can be exponentially more important than your own. This book addresses every aspect of what makes a great team and how that team can achieve major change.

If You're a Design Stakeholder

You don't know a thing about design, but somehow you've been roped into a project that hinges on it, and you're going to go in swinging. What you need to know is how you can best support the people who do this for a living by learning what they need and what to expect out of them when they're at their best. What they care about and why. What actions they might take to get to a great end product. You don't need to know exactly how they do it. You need to know what each aspect of the process achieves, what each type of designer does, the effect each skill creates, and why it matters. This book lays it all out for you.

It doesn't matter what your role is; it matters that you want to know what a great designer looks like, how to be one, or how to work with one in the best way to achieve the best outcomes.

This book shows you what "great designer" means.

▶ Inside: The Things No One Tells You

I've never attended a design school (they didn't have them when I started in the web industry), but I was involved in the first draft of a design school curriculum. This happened because I was just as fed up as every other design lead at the time over the less-than-knowledgeable students coming out of design schools and making their way to the interview table. This wasn't necessarily the fault of the students. It was often the fault of their instructors. When a person stops designing and starts teaching, their skills sometimes fall behind. The definitions and focuses of the Internet's roles and endless niches move too quickly for someone to drop out and expect to have a complete understanding of any of it even a year later. The fresh-out-of-school junior designers were walking into corporate offices everywhere without even knowing how to upload files to a server. So-called "UX designers" were lugging around copies of OmniGraffle and preaching status quo processes to companies who were as uninitiated as they were. It had to stop. So a bunch of people got together and wrote an online curriculum to be adopted by any design school that wanted it. There for the taking. They called it WaSP InterACT (WaSP is short for "Web Standards Project") (the latest version is at http://m.interactwithwebstandards.com/curriculum), and it's chock-full of good information written and compiled by very smart people.

However.

There's not a single thing in that curriculum about how designers can convince other people of their recommendations. Defend their designs. *Explain* their designs. How to know which skills a company needs out of a designer or design team. How to start with strategy and end with obsessive nitpicking only to start again two minutes later. How to improve. How to help others improve.

To help my case, I offer up the insights of several respected design leaders and researchers who have kindly agreed to contribute *their* thoughts on these oft-ignored subjects.

If you want great design, to be a great designer, to lead a team, to lead a project, to push a company forward, then put down the design book, shut down your graphics editor, stop messing around with your wireframes for a minute, and read this book.

It has the answers no one else is talking about.

▶ Not Inside: Design Skills or Their Definitions

The art and science of design is a complicated subject. Loads of books on design can and will change your life. If you're standing in a bookstore right now, there are likely a couple of dozen of them sitting on either side of this one, each with their different angles, each with their different purposes and scopes, all of which likely have some value to you as a designer (even if you end up entirely disagreeing with some of their advice). If you want to learn about the concepts and skills of designing well—the qualities of a good design, the proper way to run a usability test, and so on—pick through some of those.

For the sake of scope, this book does not teach you how to perform user research, create wireframes, design graphics, label buttons, handle errors in a form, build inline validation, or perform any other technical aspect of design. (It has taken a tremendous amount of self-discipline *not* to talk about these things, by the way.)

It does, however, sometimes look at how these things work in the real world. You might love that book over there on sophisticated usability testing methods, but I assure you, "sophisticated" rarely happens on an actual project. So, when appropriate, I talk about what really happens and how to handle it. You may have read a dozen books on how to design. I talk about how to get your designs made. How to get past the politics, reputations, and assumptions that fight against good design every single day.

My aim is not to teach you how to design. It's to help you become a designer who can do great work and get things done. To show you how to be a leader no matter your job title. How to make change within your organization. How to get around the obstacles. Stay calm. Move forward.

But yes, you will still gain some insight into how to do the actual work of design when the constraints are bigger than you're accustomed to. Several chapters in this book describe tasks designers can do to be more effective. More persuasive. More right, more often.

You're going to spot a lot that you're not currently doing. I know this because I've worked with hundreds of designers and executives. I've watched what they do. I've seen where they fail. I've heard their complaints. I've listened to their hopes. I've paid a lot of attention to the ones who succeed. I've studied what the successful ones do that others don't. I've studied what *I've* done that has worked and failed across all my own projects.

I've also studied the people who have been able to turn things around.

The soft skills of the design profession are more important than the hard skills. You can always get better at hard skills. *Loads* of resources are available on every one of them.

But you can become great only by learning how to get past all the things standing in your way. And you can lead only by knowing what a great team looks like and how to get the best out of its members.

This book is for you.

▶ Acknowledgments

This is the part where I get all weepy. Many thanks to the following people, who are awesome and who put up with a lot of crap in the interest of putting out great books:

Robyn Thomas, development editor, who diligently kept this whole process on track and stuck with me despite my crabbiness and my sudden desire to change the whole scope of the book two weeks after starting it.

Karyn Johnson, acquisitions editor, whom I'd wanted to work with *forever*, and who somehow managed to get my strange idea for a book through the acquisitions process and into readers' hands.

Scout Fest, copyeditor, who did an immaculate job and turned things around faster than I could write more words.

Liz Welch, proofreader, whose last round of editing is just as necessary as everyone else's first round, and who treated it as such.

Mimi Heft, whose masterful touch has perfected yet another book design.

The entire Peachpit staff, because, at the time of this writing, they've been a tremendous support to me for nearly a decade, and because no matter how many times we go through all this, I still find myself working with the same people I always have. Because that's how devoted they are to each other and to this business.

Nancy Davis, editor in chief, for consistently earning the respect and admiration of everyone around her, including me, and for letting me hang out with the New Riders crew a while longer to do another book.

Jared Spool, for always having one of the greatest minds in this business, and for letting me ask it questions whenever I want.

Christina Wodtke, for being a longtime friend and one of the smartest people I know. I owe you so many favors it's a little sickening.

Stephanie Troeth, another longtime friend and confidant who was so willing to help out with her insight and perspective.

Harry Max, for generally being a genius and for filling my mind with all sorts of provocative insights about what it takes to be an excellent human being.

▶ Author Biography

Robert Hoekman Jr is a user experience (UX) strategist and writer who has authored several books and dozens of articles for a range of publications, including *Fast Company* magazine's Co.Design blog. He is a columnist for the revered motorcycle culture and lifestyle magazine *Iron & Air* (www.ironandair.com), where he is also a contributing editor. He has spoken to packed rooms at dozens of events all over the world.

Robert's talents for questioning and challenging conventional wisdom have earned him success in a myriad of professional interests, including design, product strategy consulting, freelance writing, editing, and public speaking. As a veteran of the web industry, he was among the few who preached and practiced the fledgling profession of UX before it became a household term, and is considered by many to have written several of the profession's defining guidebooks. He has an undying drive to chase what he loves, a knack for asking the questions that will get him in the door, and a relentless devotion to understanding, accuracy, and quality.

He is a lifelong drummer and has a passion for psychology, metalwork, and—as his Dutch lineage would require—building furniture. He lives in downtown Phoenix, Arizona, with his partner, Jodi, and their two large dogs, Max and Daisy.

▶ Other Books by Robert Hoekman Jr

- *Designing the Obvious, 1st Edition* (New Riders, 2006)
- *Designing the Moment* (New Riders, 2008)
- *Web Anatomy* (co-authored with Jared Spool) (New Riders, 2009)
- *Designing the Obvious, 2nd Edition* (New Riders, 2010)
- *The Tao of User Experience* (self-published, 2013)

1

Introduction

▸ Key Terms

The world of user experience (UX) know-how has some gaps in it.

Big ones.

Some skills, no one talks about. Skills that are absolutely crucial to a designer's ability to do great work. Skills that will make you successful. A leader. And which, for some reason, aren't covered in the books or websites or classes on the range of skills that make up the massive topic of user experience.

These gaps include how a designer learns how to be persuasive. How to move from the end of the process to the front. How to know what arrangement of skills is most useful in the professional world. Learning what happens when you work on a project with no budget or time. How to make people understand why design is more—so much more—complicated than pushing pixels around a screen. How to go past a single project's problems to raise the bar for the whole profession. How to lead the UX charge, whether you're a lone freelancer, a junior member of a large team, or a veteran design director. How to form good arguments. Defend your design decisions. Present your work. How to keep getting better.

Despite all the resources on great design, almost nothing explains how to be a great design *professional*. For all the schools and classes and workshops on what constitutes good UX, not one bit of formalized education focuses on how to be effective at achieving that goal. Sure, they'll teach you how to do user research. How to know which pixels to move around the screen and where to put them. How to test designs. How to track metrics. How to do iterative design in Agile environments, LEAN development cycles, and other process-oriented gobbledygook. But where's the class on how to convince people you're right? On how to get coworkers and bosses to think about design first rather than having it tacked on at the end?

Where's the workshop on confidence? On leadership? On how to become a respected UX powerhouse? How to move from junior to senior?

Where's the workshop on how to lead a design effort? How to get your great ideas to the execution phase and then execute them well?

Business schools don't teach these things. Design schools definitely don't teach them.

How sad.

With all the knowledge, the opinions, the platitudes, the mandates, the one thing every person who touches a design project really needs is the potential for greatness. And it's not processes that get you there. It's not a design trend, or a favorite font, or yet another name for problem-solving. It's people.

The right people. The right situation. The right leaders. The right skills. The right actions. The right qualities.

This book is about those things.

It's a book for those of you who want to become great, whether you're part of a team, leading a team, or pushing your company's design efforts forward in some other way. It's for those of you who generally want to make yourself better in the context of any design project, regardless of your role.

I mean that. *Regardless of your role.*

I've written this book from a big-picture perspective on whom it might affect. In it, I speak specifically to designers and design leaders. But students and instructors can learn from it as well. Small business owners and design directors alike can turn these pages and find out what qualities and skills and actions make a designer able to do great work and then make sure it gets out into the world.

Whoever you are, whatever your position in the organizational chart, whatever your title might be, if you are involved in design, whether directly or peripherally, you can benefit from this book.

But it's for designers. It's so design can improve. So there can be more of it. So more people have more chances to improve the world through design.

▶ Key Terms

I took a logic class once. One day, the professor explained that a key problem during any kind of debate—the kind of problem that gets people mad and screaming at each other—is the lack of a shared definition of a key term in the argument. You can't argue with someone about the pros and cons of living in a major city without agreeing on what makes a city "major." Even slightly different definitions can make all the difference when it comes to settling anything. A decimal point can bring down a country. Accuracy matters.

Designers, their bosses, and everyone else involved are affected fairly often by this point.

Everyone knows what a designer is. So they think. But then when it comes to talking about one—what they do, where they fit into the process, what their skills should be—no one bothers to agree on what a designer actually is. Or even asks.

In truth, "designer" is a sleek term for a messy profession. A designer isn't one thing. It's a bunch of things, some of which you do, some of which you don't. Some of which you need, some of which you only think you need.

Before we dive into all this, we need common definitions for the kind of work I'll be talking about throughout the book. These distinctions are important. Throughout this book, you'll see reference after reference to designers and their designs, UX and its practitioners. We need to agree on what they mean. What they do.

Design

"Design" means different things to different people. Unless you're a designer, it probably doesn't mean what you think it means. (This is often true even if you are one.)

You can hear it used in almost any context. It's how a sports car looks. It's the flourish and styling of a vintage vanity mirror. It's the architecture behind a sophisticated web application. It's both the interface convention and the rounded edge of your smartphone. When it's talked about by a UX professional, it's how something functions. How it's organized. How it addresses a core user need that also meets business requirements with perfect balance.

So says the dictionary, but it doesn't mean any of these things. A design, by definition, is either a plan or the documented representation of a plan. It's either the act of deciding or a reference to the decision.

The design is meant to achieve that goal.

The design is on the table.

Let's design it.

It was designed that way.

A design is not something's appearance; appearance comes after planning. A design is not flourish; flourish comes after intention. A design is not architecture; a design *documents* the architecture.

"Design" is not a light word. A lot of history, thought, mindfulness, and genius are packed into those six letters.

To reduce it to anything lighter is to reduce your potential to even less. Give it its full weight and respect, and you'll get out of it what you put into it.

When I say "design," I mean a thing that can be great but is far too often ineffective. A thing that can change the world but is far too often completely frivolous.

When I say "design," it's in reference to a thing I have great respect for, and for which you should as well. Because it's the thing you have devoted your career to, and which can make or break an organization, an idea, or a cause.

Designer

A designer, then, in the context of the UX profession, is not a person who deals in appearance, in flourish, in architecture. Designers are not people who make things pretty. They are people who plan. Designs are not lines and colors and pixels. They are plans with an intended effect. Designers are thinkers. Designs are their thoughts.

Arguably, the most important thing you can do at this point of the book, at this point of understanding what it means to be a designer, is to understand that a tremendous amount of complexity is in the profession of design.

You are not a kid with a copy of Photoshop. Your purpose is not to draw lines and color them in. You are not a failed artist who signed up to be a graphic designer so you could make decent money until your real work goes viral.

A designer is a person with a big responsibility.

If you are one, your job is to think through every detail of a company's website or web product, its users, its stakeholders, its purpose, its potential. To do research, form theories, develop ideas, vet them, collaborate with others to implement them, measure them, change them.

If you are a design leader—and you will be—your job is to educate, mentor, keep your eye on the big picture, *form* the big picture, and do work in a way that is compatible with the constraints of the situation.

User Experience (UX)

"User experience" is a loaded term as well. Understandably so. As you'll see in the next chapter, the idea of what a designer is has changed a lot over the past decade or two, and "user experience" has shifted right along with it. For civilians, it's come to mean the experience they have with a product. For most people who aren't designers but who deal with them, it's come to mean "designer." This is true because, for some designers—the occasional designer who has simply shifted into UX by way of a history of graphic design and almost nothing else—UX has come to mean a way to make more money. Just throw the title into your résumé or portfolio and get a higher rate whether you're a champ at it or not. Anyone can "do UX" these days.

Of these groups of people, the civilians are the only ones who are really right.

A user's experience can't be designed. No matter how good you are at planning an intended outcome, an *experience* is far too complex, nuanced, subjective, and personal to be planned. The experience belongs to the user. No one else.

What UX people do is *influence*.

On purpose.

If any detail of a design goes without thought, the designer behind it has wasted his or her influence.

So what, then, does "user experience" mean?

UX is the application of psychology to the design of technology.

It means researching businesses and people. Thinking through the needs of both. Planning the purpose, vision, scope, feature set, design criteria, and success metrics of an entire product or a single task flow. It means testing, and validating, and plotting, and collaborating, and generally running through a bunch of different activities to sort out the best way to arrive at the conclusion everyone wants: a good experience.

A person who does this for a living is usually a devotee of all these things. An analyzer. A thinker. A problem-solver. It's not the color of the buttons that gets a UX professional invested. It's the reason for the button. Why it's there in the first place. What it will do for a user. A business. A society.

Some buttons have that kind of power.

UX people want to do something amazing. They want to design the world to a higher standard. Solve problems that haven't been solved. Invent things that improve the Internet. Make it more fun. Make it more empowering. Make it better in any way they can.

When I talk about UX professionals, these are the people I'm talking about. When I talk about UX, this is the purpose they are chasing.

Now that we have that clear.

2

The Shape of a Great Designer

▶ Some Designer History

▶ Unicorns: What They Are and
Why You Should Be One

▶ T-Shaped People: The Case for Specialties

▶ The Depth of UX

There are two perceptions: what a designer is, and what a lot of people outside the profession *think* a designer is, mostly because it used to be true, and people are terrible at noticing when things change.

In their defense, it's hard to decipher what a designer does these days.

"*Designer*" has been a moving target.

▶ Some Designer History

In the '90s, web designers were almost unknown. Programmers and executives made most of the decisions. Then the Internet grew, executives figured out they were bad at design, and left it almost entirely to the programmers, still occasionally sticking their noses in and mandating how buttons should be labeled and what feature should come next whether it made sense or not. Then designers started popping up more and more, screaming and clawing their way into the engineering-centric process as an afterthought, gritting their teeth and praying for the day their good ideas would be heard in advance, complaining about all the bad decisions in the meantime. Few of them knew anything about UX. User experience (UX) wasn't a thing yet. Nor was its predecessor, Interaction Design. Designers' great ideas were basically vapor, based on nothing more than design trends or something they thought was cool, but at least they could be inventive and raise the bar for graphical quality. They wrote front-end code, they struggled to learn JavaScript, they spent hours in Photoshop. They waited around for content to be sent to them. They designed web pages without it, filled with placeholder text. (These pages invariably broke after the real content was plugged in because CSS wasn't a thing yet either.) Anything the programmers or executives needed that might involve a photo or a font or a hyperlink (they still called them that in those days) started with "Give it to the designer!" and ended with "Why isn't it done yet?" They were a jack-of-all-trades type of designer—undervalued, underpaid, overworked, attempting to excel in five different aspects of design all at once and still be proficient at writing production code. And they ate it up. It was the Internet. It was the Wild West. It was climbing Everest. It was defining a profession, a new kind of commerce, a new world.

This person doesn't exist anymore. Not in title anyway. And a whole lot of things have happened on the way to redefining "designer."

Design has become a hundred different topics.

This all kicked off when "websites" started to become "web applications," morphing from static content to task-based experiences. "Designers" suddenly had a lot more to know. So they split into subgroups.

The Problem with Names

The first major split around this time, arguably, was the one between graphic design, web design, information architecture, and something called interaction design. Where graphic designers focused on aesthetics, "web designers" focused on front-end development, information architects focused on content and information organization, and interaction designers (IxDs) focused on function. It was no small event. We all had to start calling ourselves one thing or the other because the world lives and dies by its professional titles. A lot of people went the way of the graphic designer or web designer. The information architects, who were pretty focused in the first place, mostly remained in those roles. A few went into interaction design. (I was one of them.) Companies, practitioners, and everyone else in the world suddenly had to figure out what this new profession was all about, what its practitioners did, how their work affected things, how to tell when one was competent, how much to pay them, how to explain their roles at dinner parties.

Problem was, there was no great definition of interaction design in those days, only people trying to come up with one. Drop into any discussion on the subject and you'd think people didn't do the work, they just argued about it.

The more this went on, the less anyone could muster up a clear definition, the more employers had trouble finding an IxD whose skills matched what they needed. If they even *knew* what they needed. They may have heard about the value of an IxD, but few had any idea what one did. Or how. If IxDs couldn't explain it, how could anyone else?

It was a slow process. Some people are still fighting it out on the forums to this day. People like to define the world according to their own behaviors and beliefs. If you want to call yourself an interaction designer, simply define interaction design as whichever chunk of the work you want to do. There's no agreement. (This is made even worse by the fact that information architects often do exactly the same things interaction designers do. The titles are *almost* interchangeable, except on projects that actually involve a good amount of information design.)

So it went. So it goes. For years and years, people have been employed, and still are, with "interaction design" in their job titles whose job descriptions hardly resemble each other.

The problem then was that interaction design was totally unpredictable. Some made wireframes. Some went straight to code. Some did research. Some did usability tests. Some spent a lot of time creating "persona" descriptions and other soft deliverables that took hours to explain. Some did this or that or something else. It was rare to find two who performed the same list of design activities in the same way.

As such, the outcomes of their work compared to what people expected were erratic at best.

And Then More Showed Up

Along came the *usability analyst* (UA). It's a profession we very much needed, and they'd already been lurking around in the shadows for a little while. This was the moment they got steam.

Executives realized the designers didn't know everything after all. And they had a fairly extreme reaction. A lot of companies hired people with master's degrees in cognitive psychology and paid them copious amounts of cash to evaluate designs by way of expensive usability sessions run in labs with two-way mirrors, recording equipment, and a microphone so people could lurk behind the glass and have their minds blown by just how little anyone knew about how to make a web page actually do its job of making the company more money. Until usability professionals came along, product pages on eCommerce sites were effective *maybe* 10 to 20 percent of the time—on a good day. People visited the same page over and over before finally committing to a purchase, and even then, they frequently abandoned the shopping cart process when it threw error after error at them, and that was when they were lucky enough to get through the first two pages without their session expiring.

Oh yeah. It was the good ol' days.

Usability pros helped change all that. They started sorting out ways to measure a page's effectiveness, a user's satisfaction level, the difficulty of doing so. They set up cameras, paid people $50 a pop to try out a design, and asked them questions like, "How would you rate the ease of this task on a scale of 1 to 10, with 10 being the toughest?" They marked down when people couldn't get through a task at all. They called them "hard stops." Not the kind of thing you want hear. (They've found ways to be better and faster since then. More on that in Chapter 3.)

After a while, UAs established themselves. Some great people wrote some great books about web usability to help it along, and things were looking smooth for a minute. Then people started to realize the job of a designer should be to design better in the first place so that this stuff would stop happening. Designers all around dove into research—into thinking before speaking, as it were. And *interaction design* became too limited a term.

The Birth of the User Experience Designer

So another split happened.

We weren't just designing function. We were doing research. We were talking with users, reviewing competing products, interviewing stakeholders, and defining strategies for web *app* design. We took all the knowledge and insight from this process and used it to determine the scope of an *application*, its feature set, its task flows, its layouts, its everything. Then we designed function. How the site or product worked was the result, but a bunch of skills went into the why and how of that function. We didn't design cool things. We defined *reasons* for designing cool things.

That's not interaction design, we said. That's *user experience design*. We were considering the whole, not just the pieces.

The more we considered the whole, the more we once again started to dig deeper into the individual skills to find how far they went. User research, for example, is a deep subject. So is competitive analysis. And stakeholders (a subject unto themselves)? Well, they all have different ideas about what's important and why, and getting people with competing or conflicting stakes in a web application to agree on the overarching vision for a site can be a full-time job. Hence, we needed a separate title. We needed something to split this more complete approach from the more traditional practice of interaction design.

The name change was justified. This was UX Design. Holistic. All-encompassing. Long-view stuff.

The problem is, we left "design" at the end of it.

Stupid, stupid, stupid.

Design Is a Four-Letter Word

"Design" conjures up notions of all things visual—the way things look when they're finally finished. This was fine for interaction designers, because the result was in fact visual (and functional). Let's face it, we rarely had the opportunity to do any real research on projects like we imagined we would, so the activities we performed to get there were almost all visual. Really, all we were doing was making wireframes and prototypes and calling it interaction design, knowing full well how much more thorough it *should* be. Interaction designers spent most of their time fighting for the chance to do interaction design.

It was even worse for UX designers. We had to start from scratch. We were yet another kind of designer for employers to make sense of and pay. But hey, at least we were still doing "design" work.

We did this for a reason.

The word "design" helped people grok the new niche. In theory. But it also had a few negative effects.

First, it tricked people into thinking about visual design and not the kind of design we were actually attempting to do: the *planning* kind. So UX designers have spent an insane amount of time trying to convince people their jobs are a lot more than visual and interaction design. All along, part of the problem has been sitting right there in the job title—UX *design*.

Second, UX *design* convinced people who design in any capacity that they, too, can or should refer to themselves as UX designers regardless of whether or not they can dance with one foot in a good number of UX skills.

There's a huge advantage in doing so, of course. UX designers get paid more.

Third, it created some confusion between UX design and UI design (user interface design). UI design, many argued, is basically a UX designer without the strategic part of the job. You design interfaces—actual screens— plain and simple. They've also argued that UI is a subset of UX. (They'd be right, by the way. UX is the umbrella for UI, IxD, IA, visual design, usability testing, and whatever else you can come up with that affects a user's experience.)

Countless other title divisions have occurred along the way. Getting into all of them and what they mean would take half the book. I'm sticking to the major ones.

So during the first half of the 2010s, a great many UX designers—especially younger ones, newer to the profession—were more like graphic designers and/or coders who had committed to a focus on usability.

This undercuts the entire notion of UX. Although graphic design, usability, and code all have a *massive* effect on the user's experience, they are all but pieces of the UX pie. Actually, I don't even want to say they're pieces of the pie for fear of implying that the pie is made up of these elements. It's not. These things are the mere *serving utensils* of the UX pie. And yet here they were, doing tiny slivers of a broad and deep profession.

People with years of experience doing research and strategy definition and people with years of experience (or not) doing little more than graphic design were both calling themselves "UX designers."

The Rebirth of the Nebulous Job Title

Despite all the effort to define this new title, its practical everyday usage dictated its own meaning right back at us. We wanted it to mean research and strategy. It ended up meaning some combination of UI design, information architecture, user research, front-end coding, or more. Or less. Depends on who you ask, and who has the job title.

So we've ended up with all-encompassing titles once again. We started with the almighty "designer." Now we have the almighty "UX designer."

This time, though, we have a truckload of skills and alternative job titles alongside it that no one really understands. UX designers can do it all, but within companies that are still trying it all on for the first time, it now takes an obscene amount of time to explain and justify everything they can (and should) do and to fight for the influence to do it.

Basically, we forgot to study history. We named another profession, set about defining it, screwed it up beyond belief, sent all sorts of mixed messages about what it means, and started writing our new self-claimed job titles on our business cards willy-nilly and heading off on the conference circuit to have expensive dinners together thanks to our new, much higher paychecks.

Confuse and disorient. Sometimes, that's the key to getting a raise, apparently. If you want to make more money, invent a job title, fail to define it, and convince everyone they're missing it.

In short: "UX design" is a common term, and no one has any idea what it means. It's come to imply something either very specific or very general. Someone who does it all. And the term does nothing to weed out the newbies from the veterans.

Design schools now regularly churn out UX designers, most of whom have some combination of design skills and some level of competency in each one. And depending on the school, these designers can be decently talented. Solid, even. After all that hyper-specialization that occurred for such a long time, there's enough shared knowledge now that it's approachable and accessible to a lot more people than the specialists. It's much easier to be good now at a bunch of different things. And this time, *good* means a lot more than it did it in the '90s. A basic level of knowledge in a range of subjects is often enough to get by. You may not be amazing at any of them, but you can certainly do solid work.

But the job title is still as nebulous as it gets. User Experience Designer can mean almost anything and be uttered by almost anyone with a laptop. Companies struggle to find the right people. Students struggle to nurture the right skills. Designers struggle to find the right situations and get ahead.

The problems with this term are going to last for years. It's going to get worse.

We could try to kill it off completely—divide it up a little more so we can at least dole out some appropriate job titles. But it's a fight not worth having. We'll never win it. People will call themselves what they want. Others will buy into it or not.

To me, "UX design" is a ridiculous term. But I'm conceding the battle here and now. I concede that I may just be defining the world according to my own behaviors and beliefs. I give up. And I don't care. Call yourself what you want. Better to follow the question "What do you do?" with "And what does that mean to you?" Better to decide what makes a designer great and then teach the world, and ourselves, to look for it.

No matter what I think, it's one of the biggest problems we have as a profession. "UX design" means everything and nothing. We can't explain it. Companies can't understand it.

But they do know what they want.

Ask any hiring manager in the business what they need from a UX designer these days and you'll almost universally get the same answer:

We want unicorns.

▶ Unicorns: What They Are and Why You Should Be One

Companies want people who do it all.

Whatever we call them these days, designers aren't "designers" anymore. They do a lot more than design. Nor are they niche expects. They do a whole bunch of things that fall outside of any single discipline.

Designers are now "UX designers." They're collections of skill sets and weird job titles with disputed meanings and overlapping responsibilities and activities no one can seem to make any sense out of whatsoever but all of which are necessary. And although their titles mostly point to single aspects of design, a lot of them have at least some competency in a whole bunch of different disciplines, and they jump from one to the next on any given day depending on the needs of the project.

They're generalists. They're unicorns.

Unicorn = Generalist

Sometimes called a "purple squirrel" for its equally mythical state, a unicorn is the person most like the one I described in the beginning of this chapter—the crazy ambitious designer who worked in the Wild West and did everything for everyone. For a long time, people like this were commonly considered a rarity. Now they're coming up all over the place. And there's a need for them. And for good reason:

Companies don't need full-time specialists most of the time. Rarely do companies need enough usability testing for someone to do it full time. And rarely do they require enough content strategy for a permanent person to take it on. Instead, companies need overlap. They need a group of people who have a range of skills. People who can do user research and strategy definition, swing into interaction design and content strategy, maybe kick up a prototype or two along the way (in one form or another), run usability tests at a couple of stages, and *maybe* even help out with visual design. Companies want students who can come out of school knowing how to do all these things (to some degree at least) and who are dying to get better at all of it. They want teams that can switch between priorities on a dime, move in all directions, and get it all done.

They also want generalists because no matter what, you the designer will find yourself maxed out at some point. Your particular set of skills will be needed on other projects, and you'll have no time to give to them. If three other people on your team can do some of the same work you can, a director can get them slinging their skills on the other stuff.

Be Replaceable

Before we move on, let's talk about the thing that just popped into your head: Redundancy on a team makes it sound like you're replaceable.

You are. You should be.

No matter how good you are or how well you fill a niche, or how useful you are in whatever situation comes up in a day, you are replaceable.

This should comfort you. You need to be replaceable.

If you're absolutely perfect for one thing, you're less perfect for a bunch of other things. It'll be harder for you to find the perfect job. It'll be hard to find *any* job. If you're replaceable, you're hirable. Besides that, you want to be able to move on at some point. Test out your other skills. Develop new ones. Work on a different product you care about more than this one. If you're replaceable, a company won't trap you into staying by throwing more and more money at you until it's impossible for you to leave. Every job eventually turns into the wrong situation, whether because the job changes or because you do. The web industry isn't built for lifers. It's built for people with an endless sense of adventure. An incessant will to take on the next project. The next challenge. When that feeling strikes, you need to be able to leave. Don't get trapped by money. Make too much cash in one place for that perfect thing you do, and your desire to get out will drive you mad.

There's also the reality of emergencies. You're a human being, and you're going to experience a few of them. A health emergency. A car accident on a day full of deadlines. A death in the family. Sick kid. You name it. You need to be able to take a day off, a week, three weeks, and not spend that time worrying about what you're not getting done. Let it get done by someone else. No UX project will ever be more important than your life.

Be replaceable.

The Upside of Overlap

Now back to the topic at hand:

Another reason companies need generalists is so they can teach each other. We've all heard that small teams are more effective than individuals. No individual can think of everything, do everything, know everything. Teams make people better. When the people on those teams share skills, they collectively have the benefit of shared interest. They read different articles, different books, go to different conferences and local events. You bring those insights back to the group and share them. You learn from each other. You change each other's minds. You get the benefit of multiple perspectives. You get the benefit of debate.

This is great for a company. It's great for the products you're working on. It's fantastic for users, because it's not a single-minded effort that brings a product into their lives, but a collaborative, considered, deliberate effort managed by a group of people who come up with more ideas, poke holes in more arguments, anticipate more problems, and solve more issues before they get out onto the Internet.

And that's just the corporate world.

Small businesses always need a good unicorn or two.

Let's say you're a small business owner. A lone accountant, a fish store owner, a hair stylist, a restaurateur. You need a website, but cheap and uncomplicated. A few pages about your business, a contact form.

Jack-of-all-trades generalists make for great freelancers. And they often like to bundle basic services together. They can set up a website for you with a relatively usable content management system on the back side so you can make your own updates. They can handle web hosting for you. They can help you pick a "theme" (a canned website design—one of a billion out there—that works for a wide range of purposes), customize it a bit, handle all the hosting issues, and then charge you a single monthly rate for all of it. The only time you need to bug this person again is when you want significant changes made. Otherwise, you can let it sit there doing its job for a long time to come.

For now, these people are called unicorns. Eventually, that will stop.

Jared Spool and Dr. Leslie Inman have seen this coming. Their design school, Centre Center, was originally called The Unicorn Institute. They had to change the name prior to its launch because the term isn't sustainable. "While [the title is] cute right now," Jared says, "it won't be cute a decade from now. If we do what we want to do well, then the workforce we're creating, in essence, won't be unicorns." But its goal is definitely the same. It features a curriculum that has its students working on real projects, with real outcomes. Over the course of two years, students learn a range of skills, all of which help them become valuable to companies after they graduate.

What will we call them? We'll call them "designers" again. And with any luck, there will be loads of them. Unicorns will no longer be on the endangered list. Everyone will be some variation of a UX professional. "Design" will refer once again to the entire collection of skills, and these skills will mean a lot more than they used to. And companies will have all the skill overlap they need.

Be Respectful

Christina Wodtke backs up the idea that everyone should know something about everyone else's skills. For one very key reason:

It helps people respect each other.

Christina has been the GM of Social at MySpace, Principal Product Manager at LinkedIn, GM at Zynga, and publisher of revered web magazine *Boxes and Arrows*. She has also been involved with countless startups as a Silicon Valley veteran, and was even responsible for the seminal book *Information Architecture: Blueprints for the Web* (2nd Ed., New Riders, 2009). If anyone can talk about what makes designers great, it's Christina. (Note: I consulted on the second edition of Christina's *Information Architecture: Blueprints for the Web*, but I do not earn royalties on it.)

She points to a lack of respect as one of the biggest mistakes a designer can make.

> *I would say the one thing that I really badly want and I hate to say it's rare, but it is, and it kills me that it's rare, is genuine respect for other disciplines.*

Big companies, especially, tend to have multiple designers, and when that happens, they tend to stick together and forget to fall in love with all the other aspects of the things they're designing. She continues:

> *I meet so many designers who just don't understand and don't care what their engineer does, or what their product manager does, or what a general manager does, or what marketing does, and those are most often the people who say, "How do I get people to respect me?" And—well—as well as being respectable: respect others. I would hope that designers would have a sense of curiosity. Would want to dig into how these other people live their lives, and yet, very often they just stay inside their little designer bullpen. They all go to lunch together, and they all sit together, they all leave at the same time.*

I second this idea. Big time. Understanding the depth of someone else's work—its difficulties, its stresses—can do amazing things for your ability to get work done. Always taking their constraints into consideration, collaborating with them during projects, getting to know them as people, having those great hallway conversations with them after normal work hours can make a good project great. Chemistry, rapport, *respect*. These things will change your life.

And actively *dis*respecting the people around you can crush your rapport with everyone *else* on the team. Never—ever—assume you know what someone else is dealing with. If that person is the go-to on a subject, never assume you can do it better than they can. Odds are, you know only enough about it to suck and have no idea just how much.

If that point isn't sinking in just yet, don't worry, I make it again later on in this book.

Moving on.

In a tremendous number of circumstances, generalists are the perfect combination of good-enough skills to do solid work. You don't *need* deep expertise. You *need* someone who's competent. Competence is good enough for a lot of situations. Most, even. Talented is nice. Skilled and experienced are fantastic. But specialism? You don't need it all the time.

Until you do.

▶ T-Shaped People: The Case for Specialties

There's a problem with generalists.

To the naked eye, it looks like the Internet is chock-full of expertise. And it is, really. For every hyper-niche topic you can think to research, the Internet has a major archive of articles on it. Whether they're well researched and insightful or trite and full of link-bait platitudes is a different story, but rest assured, they're out there. What's the best alignment for form labels? What do people really think about drag-and-drop?

Do drop-down menus really have a lower level of usability? What's the best way to do user research? Whatever the subject, a whole world of opinion-loaded content is out there on just what you need to know, most of which borrows heavily from something else on the subject.

Let's be honest. When was the last time you read something *original* about UX online?

There's a clue in your answer. Something you should notice. If everyone is saying the same things, it's probably not because they all came to the same conclusions on their own. It's taken a lot of time for people to build up the UX know-how that designers can now all take for granted. Those articles have been stacking up for a long time. Long enough that these days you can start writing your own articles after reading just a few of the existing pieces. A couple of weeks on the web and you could reasonably pawn yourself off as a consultant. (Eh. You'd get called out pretty quickly, though, unless you worked with a client who had no UX knowledge at all.)

Each subtopic has become more evolved, more complicated, but we've learned so much about every aspect of design, content, research, usability, that we can skim the surface and do reasonably well. Being competent at any one of these skills now takes a lot less time than it used to. Day One of UX practice means standing on the shoulders of a whole bunch of people who came before.

It all came from somewhere.

It came from people devoting their careers over the past 10, 15, 20 years to getting better and better at some niche part of the profession and then spending years talking about it at conferences and writing articles and books. Working with clients. Researching. Digging deep. *Becoming specialists.*

That's where most of the knowledge comes from. Specialists dig it up and then give it away.

Expertise is like bird food. Someone has to go get it and bring it back to the others. When everyone's a generalist, there's no expertise.

Generalists, however competent, are masters of nothing. *Specialists* are the people who generate the breadth and depth of knowledge that generalists feed on to survive.

In other words, we need them. Badly.

We need people to dive deep, pull out the great insight, and simplify it so everyone else can benefit from it.

You should be one.

Sometime, somehow, after you've gotten a solid handle on the range of skills that'll make you employable or able to freelance your way into building your own agency, I hope you pick a specialty.

I hope you pick several of them, in fact. I hope you dive deep into as many topics as you can so you're more than a passable practitioner, but a veteran in all aspects of your profession. Becoming a generalist with several areas of expertise will make you incredibly useful to the profession.

The trouble is, you can't. At least not all at once. You can do it over the course of your career, but out of the gate, you can only specialize so much and still keep up on your generalist skills.

Becoming a T-Shaped Person

But please do become a specialist.

Pick a specialty and learn everything you can about it. Become a T-shaped person.

My favorite kind of person.

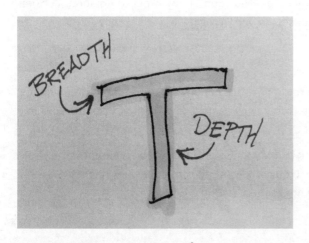

A T-shaped person is just what it sounds like. The horizontal top line is a set of skills in which you have reasonable understanding and knowledge, and the upright center line is a single skill in which you have significant depth. For example, you might be decent at whipping up wireframes, prototyping in code, research, and usability testing, but when it comes to strategy definition, you are a master. And because of that, you're invaluable to a company.

Although a great many people can do a great many things, few of them are great at anything until they specialize in something.

Besides being able to bring some new expertise to a subject area and share it with the world, specialization in at least one subject makes you incredibly employable.

When companies need deep knowledge, they need to have some specialists around to bring it. If you can demonstrate that you know your stuff, you can become the go-to for your subject.

Besides all that, being well rounded means never getting to a point of greatness. Never seeing what you can do at your best. So sad. Yes, you can be an extraordinary generalist, and you can certainly be valued for that. But digging deep into one discipline is an unbeatable experience. And it's for the most counterintuitive reason you can imagine:

It means you can finally understand how little you know.

Designers work along a spectrum. In the beginning, they complain a lot. Bad design eats at them, but they don't know what to do about it. Soon, they start trying to take them on. They get a few wins. They start to believe they're pretty good.

Really good.

There's no evidence to support this notion, of course, but they don't know that yet. They have no *other* evidence to compare their work to. No frame of reference. Not yet.

Time goes by, they look back at their prior work, and realize it was terrible. If they're lucky, they realize the work they're doing now might be terrible to them a year from now.

If they're smart, they do something about it. They start studying the ways other people go about this deceptively complex and difficult work. They learn new methods. Grow. Expand their knowledge. They make a few (dozen) mistakes. They get a few wins. Wins they can prove. The wins stack up.

Eventually, they start to see something they couldn't possibly have seen at the beginning: when they're right and when they're not. They learn to distinguish. They realize—slowly—how little they knew before. They realize something pivotal:

How much they still don't know.

In the beginning, they were people who "knew enough to be dangerous," as it were. And man was it ever true.

The ego they had before slips away.

Now they're on the path to *actually* being really good.

You only know it all in the beginning. The more you learn, the more that feeling fades away. A new one shows up: the feeling of knowing how lucky you are to have picked a profession you can never master. How glad you are there's always something new to learn. Always a chance to improve.

That this profession will never get boring.

When you get far enough along the spectrum that you *really* know the difference between bad and good, and how much there is to know, and that you will always be surprised, and are convinced you're nothing more than mediocre—that's when you're at your best. That's when you get the best results. You've put in your 10,000 hours. You've become the person everyone considers a master. Conversely, you wake up knowing there is no such thing. You're only a master because you never stop learning.

If you're a design professional, this is the point you want to get to.

Masquerading as a Generalist

In my career, since "UX" became a thing, I've noticed an ugly trend that grates against this sensibility of becoming a solid generalist with a deep knowledge in at least one discipline. And it's troubling, because it leads to a sort of false UX, and perpetuates the confusion wrapped around the whole notion of what a UX professional is supposed to be and do.

It's a specialist disguised as a generalist. A specialist who refers to himself as a *UX designer,* but who really does not have the breadth of skills or UX understanding to qualify himself of that title.

It seems to happen either when schools fail to live up to their job of teaching a breadth of skills, or when junior designers who have a limited set of abilities try to reach beyond their skill sets, whether out of ambition or a misguided perspective. A graphic designer, for example, who has started doing wireframes and thinks this is all it takes to become a UX designer.

You can't really blame him. UX, after all, pays better.

But this isn't UX. Not to the depth it deserves.

▶ The Depth of UX

UX work is planning work. We're not designing a user's experience, we're planning for it. Trying to influence it. We're creating the conditions in which a person can have an experience. A certain *kind* of experience—the kind in which we hope that people will have certain kinds of emotions, will perform certain kinds of behaviors, and through which they will achieve certain outcomes that help us achieve our own desired outcomes. If the goal is to entertain, it's the kind of experience people are entertained by. If the goal is to support and encourage a specific, productive activity, it's the kind of experience wherein a person can complete that activity without distraction and with an appropriate amount and type of cognitive friction. We're planning for people to be able to walk away feeling smart, productive, and respected. Confident. Like they understand what just happened.

This "experience" is wrapped up in how the user feels that day. It's dependent on how a person feels about a company, whether having just heard about it five seconds ago or ten years ago. It's mixed up in how a person feels about the customer support call they made once. The ads they've seen. The kinds of people they know who like the company or its product (because product relationships are as much about self-identity as the product itself).

It's at least partly insane for a person to think he or she can *design* a user's experience, let alone that it can be done by way of a single skill within such a broad thing as UX. A user's experience can't be addressed by spending 70 percent of our time in a graphics editing program. If anything, we should spend 70 percent of our time in a psychologist's office and library, neck-deep in studies and psychoses, and only after a few years of this should we even be allowed to consider affecting a user's experience, let alone believe we can do it adeptly. In even postulating the idea that we can design a user's experience, we discredit the incredible complexity and range of the very subject UX professionals dedicate themselves to.

Photoshop doesn't have "Confidence" and "Understanding" menu options. Code editors don't have "Loyalty" and "Satisfaction" options. Experiences can't be composed strictly through graphics, nor can they be coded with HTML. These aspects of design have a *massive* impact on the experience the user will ultimately have, but they have next to nothing to do with crafting the very nature of the experience we claim to be facilitating.

No.

That happens in understanding a company's purpose, it's hope, how it wishes to be perceived, how it hopes to fit into its customers' lives, what value its customers (people!) should see in it, how they should feel about it, how often and in what ways they'll use it, how important it will be to them, and on and on and on. It is through this understanding, and only through this understanding, that we are able to achieve the true and noble aims of user experience. We have to gain this understanding, translate it into a picture of the kind of experience we hope people will have (now and later), identify the qualities of that experience and what we can do to achieve them, and then take steps to create an environment in which that kind of experience is most likely to result for most people, most of the time.

User experience work is not just about making things easy. It's a balancing of human psychology, the requirements of a given situation, and the qualities of various types of experiences (productive, immersive, entertaining, exploratory, and so on) in an effort to offer a set of circumstances wherein users can have an experience beneficial to both themselves and to the organization.

UX is far more rooted in psychology than graphic design. It starts with research, rounds out with a defined vision, and ends with a plan.

UX covers a lot of skills and activities, few of which actually come out as anything a user will ever see or touch, but all of which go far beyond any single skill. Mostly, UX deliverables are descriptions and summaries and strategy documents and prototypes and diagrams and lists. It's research and thought. UX practitioners deal in strategy. When someone spends more time designing graphics than developing a big-picture perspective of a sophisticated situation, they're not practicing UX.

Design is the application of a strategy. This is not to say it's somehow "the easy part," because it definitely is not. Graphic design is every bit as hairy as any other practice centered on the implicit and explicit manipulation of human emotion and behavior (and this, quite frankly, is the result of any kind of design, however noble the purpose of the thing doing the manipulating). But there is a vast disciplinary difference between UX and any single aspect of it. These individual skills are all born in the same jungle, but UX is the jungle itself. All these skills are part of it. They all affect it.

UX work is a strategic exercise, whereas design is how strategic muscle is applied—it's where strategy gets its elbows greased.

We cannot properly develop the intended experience by putting items on a screen and considering their structure, layout, tone, message, and so on in hopes that intention might leap out at us. These things must come after the intention is defined, and the intention *must* be defined, else graphic design is a meaningless act.

None of this is to say we should deride these people who are masquerading as generalists.

They are in fact quite valuable, so much so that I'm not sure this profession would be able to make the progress it has, or continue, without them. Many organizations can justify only a very small team of people, if even more than one person alone, to do this work. A usability-minded graphic designer is a far better UX professional than none at all, and one with a decent level of interest in reading the relevant sites and books on usability and UX can as a result do a decent job of UX-centric thinking much of the time. I would never suggest we boot these people out on the basis that they fall short of some high ideal of true UX. I'll leave that to the semantic purists.

Quite the opposite, we should help them *improve* their grasp of this type of thinking and point them in the right direction to keep learning. The world needs more UX professionals, and there is a slew of people with graphic design and/or coding skills sitting at the dining table, forks and knives in hand, ready to stab into any piece of meat that looks like it might fill their hunger. To deny them such a meal for any reason would be a serious injustice and would only serve to hurt the UX profession.

We can help them become generalists. We can help them find their specialties. Later on, they can help *everyone* create the better world all the designers are really after.

In the meantime:

Clearly, there's no way to know exactly what a UX professional does or knows or believes through a job title alone. "UX designer" is vague and meaningless at best. "Interaction designer" may have been better, but its definition also depends just as much on who you ask as who's doing the job.

That's the lesson.

No matter what title you choose or come across, it has to be qualified by looking at the actual skill set of the individual. Titles mean nothing without their asterisks.

And regardless of what we call them, whether a designer has been around for twenty years or just walked out of design school, odds are that person is pretty great at some things, mediocre at others. D-school doesn't cover it all. Neither does experience. Some things have to be pointed out. Like how to be persuasive. How to be right and prove it. How to be more efficient and effective. A lot more. And you can be amazing at any or all of these skills and still fail, for example, thanks to a total lack of rhetorical know-how.

So let's talk about what makes designers effective.

3

Adapting

▶ Tools, Not Processes

▶ Improvising

▶ Working Quickly

Rigidity is almost a hallmark of UX debates. It should be the opposite.

It started in the early days of referring to this kind of work as interaction design. Designers would congregate on discussion lists and ask questions and debate everything from which was the best wireframe software to whether or not designers should be required to write code (only enough to know what you're talking about and to produce HTML prototypes). It was rare that anyone came to any conclusions. What seemed to matter most was being right.

What should have mattered most was the *debate*.

Debate is important. It helps the design world move. You can either take part and push your agenda, your ideology, your insight, or you can sit back and listen to what everyone says about a subject and try a few things yourself until you start to form your own opinion on the matter.

Of course, a lot of debates are useless. Like the ones on subjects that are provable.

Like the one about process.

Designers love their process debates. It's practically a national pastime on the forums. On blogs. In web magazines. One designer after another storms onto the Internet and announces the superiority of one process after another. Some of these designers are well known. They're conference speakers. Book authors. The heads of respected design agencies. Others are unknowns, six months into their first real job, eager to make a name for themselves and relying on the first approach they tried. And the web lets them do it. You don't have to have a big name to write an article that gets published by a major online magazine about web design. You just have to have a good pitch. (You can pick the writers out, too. They're the ones who write the longest articles, use passive voice a lot, and link to a dozen things you've already read. But I digress.) Every so often, someone writes a book about one. When these articles and books are convincing, people latch on to them, practice them for a minute, then rehash the ideas into yet more articles. Honestly, it's exhausting. On any given day now, it takes more time to get through the list of new articles about UX than it takes to write one worth reading (check the #UX hashtag on Twitter sometime to see what I mean). But again, debate is good. It takes a lot of voices to move the needle, and when it works, it's a great thing. It's progress.

Few articles on process will ever end with progress.

The subject has been studied. The situation has been lived out by countless designers. Consultants (like me), who work with a dozen different companies every year, see it firsthand.

It's provable.

You can argue about it all you want. Throw around baseless mandates about how it should be done. Try to mold the world according to your worldview (as we all do) only to have it kick you in the back of the head later. But if you actually *study* the situation, three things become pretty clear.

Process is crap. Improvisation is essential. And designers stuck on traditional and formal methods are useless in the field.

Designers—good designers, *experienced* designers, designers who produce great work—don't rely on these things.

Not even a little.

▶ Tools, Not Processes

LEAN. Agile. Before that, it was User-Centered Design (UCD). (Is that still a thing? No one could ever decide whether UCD was a process or a philosophy.) Every couple of years, someone comes along, renames the old thing, and sells it like lemonade on a hot day. Suddenly, books and articles and conferences are all focusing on it. Predictably on it goes. "Design thinking" is the new "interaction design," which was the new—well, "problem solving."

No matter how it's all defined and named, thinking about it at all might not be of much value.

I'll say it again: Process is crap.

Every company has a different version of LEAN. Every startup uses a new variation of Agile. Every designer has (or had) a different definition of UCD. It's not because they don't believe in the ideas. It's just that they see the truth about things that start out as rigid, inflexible process definitions.

The definitions work only in the situation they were designed for—the one the process inventors were in when they developed it. In every other situation in the world, you have to modify them. Designers who try to stay strict to their processes drive themselves crazy.

So why are designers so hellbent on inventing and defending them? The primary argument for the rigid responders usually centers around one idea:

For designers to be successful, they must be able to repeat their successes, and process is repeatable.

Of course, it's a ridiculous argument. Process *is* repeatable, sure. But when has a *process* ever guaranteed success?

Look at the facts.

What happens when a project starts? Someone lays out who will be involved, and how much time you all have to finish the project. (Under the best circumstances, this deadline is even based on a real constraint, like how much money the startup has before it goes under, but this is true less often than you'd think.)

Time and money. Time and money. It's always time and money.

And those two variables change for nearly every project. Even looking at a project through its most basic lens of time and money, process is born to fail. We're not building cabinets for gated communities of tract houses. Our projects are all different from each other. No two are the same. You cannot shove a square process into a round project. If your version of Agile includes two weeks of lead time for research and design and a few two-week sprints, a three-week project timeline throws everything you know right out the window. It puts you in a position to work 90 hours a week. It puts you in a position to design something half as good as it could've been if only you'd had time to rest and think once in a while.

And this is what a lot of designers do. They move their beds into the office and get going and agonize for the rest of their lives over how the project could've been so much better. This is what happens every time someone tries to stay with a plan despite all the circumstances that should tell them it's a no-go.

Wasn't it Mike Tyson who said, "Everyone's got a plan till they get punched in the mouth"?

Yay, process!

What a sad thing to obsess over.

I've been working with and watching designers for a long time. Different companies. Different team setups. Different products. Different places. Know what they all have in common? Not much. They all have their own ways of thinking, their own sets of skills, their own degrees of competence. Their own bosses and stakeholders and users and complaints.

They all have their own *constraints*.

If you stand really far back and let your eyes glaze over, every project looks the same to some degree.

Up close, every project is a brand-new set of politics and problems. Far more than design work, a designer's job is to navigate. And rigidity won't help you there. It doesn't matter how design starts or how it goes. It matters how it ends. (Not that design really ends.)

When you watch a few great designers or design teams do their thing, you notice something. They don't have processes. They have *tools*. Lots and lots of tools.

Like a pool of users and stakeholders to pick from and interview. Whiteboard sketching. Rapid prototyping. Guerrilla usability testing. A fierce belief in "minimum viable product" (MVP). Smoke testing. Experience. Instincts. Data tracking. Reusable code. Frameworks. A love of collaboration. Mutual respect. Sometimes they have a conference room they can take over for the next three weeks.

After describing to me a particular team she worked with, which was full of smart and interesting people, Stephanie Troeth said:

> *Sadly, they also made one major mistake: They tried to put in layers and layers of formalized process. When you have a roomful of smart people, you have to acknowledge that they might be able to short circuit the process and arrive at a different way of working.*

(Steph is a veteran UX strategist and designer who's been involved with the Web Standards Project, and who spearheaded international design and user research for MailChimp through a four-year consulting stint with them. She's also a respected speaker and writer.)

The situation she describes is a nice example of designers getting in their own way.

Great designers don't stifle themselves with processes. They get to work.

When the constraints of the situation get spelled out and thrust upon them, process is the first thing to go. They pick and choose what and how and do it quickly. They throw down. They *adapt.*

Great designers treat every project like a new adventure, a new set of nutso factors to be beaten and handled by pulling out one skillful knife after another and carving up that project like a med-school cadaver.

They take their tools, and they do something really cool with them.

▶ Improvising

When I was a teenager, I used to go to this mountain on the north side of town before sunrise, sometimes alone, sometimes with friends. The mountain had three or four hiking trails. Depending on the day and time, they'd either be vacant or jammed full of people with walking sticks and tennis shoes and headphones. One thing never changed. The trails were all paved with asphalt. This automatically made them less appealing to me. Probably an effect of all the camping I did as a kid. The desert is always better. The dirt. The rocks. The messiness of finding your own way, inventing your own trail. So I'd stand at the bottom of the mountain, point my finger at some place higher up, and say, "There. I want to go there." And then I'd just go. I'd weave around the bushes and navigate around boulders and trees and slip a few times and scrape my calf and bang my shin into a rock and end up with raw hands. Every time, it was an experience worth having. When I hit the point I'd set out to reach, I'd sit down and stare out over my city. It was a 365-degree panoramic view of tiny buildings, cars turned into dots on nameless highways, and not a problem in sight. Problems disappear at the tops of mountains. They fade into nothing. The cuts and knocks and raw hands don't mean a thing. There's just wide open space and clear sky and taking your life back, if only for just an hour.

(Getting down was often a problem. But it was a problem for another time. After the sun came up.)

If the thought of living in mania—living without process and relying strictly on tools—doesn't appeal to you, consider this:

Anything less, and this work wouldn't be nearly so fun.

When you blow off processes and live on tools, you learn to master something not many people are great at but that is a valued skill among any kind of craftsmen (and web design is most certainly a craft). Namely, the ability to improvise.

Yet another thing they don't teach in school. Not just D-school. Any school.

Which is strange, because it's such an admired thing. It's having the wits about you to replace the busted stick shift handle in your car with a tennis ball. It's creating a shim for a wobbly table out a folded-up business card (though, are you really still carrying those things around?). It's taking advantage of a wine spill on your white carpet to paint a rug around it like it was by design. Do any of these things and the people around you will sit in admiration of your prowess for making something great out of whatever's handy.

For a lot of people, it's a hard thing to do. When a project goes awry, they get stuck. They get angry. They get stressed out. They look to others to take the lead and go home feeling like failures.

I think these are the same people who believe process is a requirement for repeatable success. (That whole idea of defining the world according to your own actions.)

It's not.

Repeatable success comes from one's ability to repeatedly improvise.

It's not just about getting through a design, either. Improvisation can get you more resources out of a slim budget. It can get you impromptu coding tests to validate someone's guesswork. It can get you through a usability test with a crashed laptop by sketching screens on napkins and stepping through a task flow anyway.

Your ability to improvise doesn't just help you. It helps the other people involved trust you. Depend on you. It makes them come to you when they can't think up what to do next.

Psychological studies have shown it's more difficult to have good ideas and make good decisions when you're under stress. Staying aloof to a certain extent can give you the brain space you need to bust out a good idea under bad circumstances. Being able to improvise shows you can keep a clear head when a project goes wrong, and approach situations with a level of calm not everyone has.

It also gives the impression of experience, even if you don't have any. So many designers leap to solutions devised in a panic. An experienced designer stays calm, shuts up for a minute, thinks through the angles and asks questions about the constraints and looks around for anything that might help in the moment, then pitches something no one else has been able to think up.

I worked with a programmer once who could do this.

I've always thought it takes a certain kind of mind to be a brilliant engineer. This guy was the poster child for it. When people got stuck, he'd sit next to them, stare at their screens for a few minutes, ask some questions, and then tell you to do something that sounded like it'd come out of left field and which worked on the first try. It was virtually the opposite of everything you'd tried. You'd spent five hours on the effort only to realize you'd been approaching it the same way the whole time and that your approach wasn't going to get you anywhere. (Granted, I was a mediocre programmer. But even if I'd tacked up five more years of experience, I'm pretty sure he'd still have been faster than I was in situations like that.)

It was downright satisfying to watch someone do this. It still is. It's the kind of thing that makes you sit back and ask, "How did you do that?"

After a bunch of years of experience, people might start asking you that question. In the meantime, you can fake it. And faking it will help you learn how to do it.

Improvisation shows competence. It shows situational awareness. It shows intelligence. It shows you truly have a grasp on a bunch of different concepts and skills, and are able to pluck them out of the sky at will, rearrange them, and make them into something new. It means you understand concepts over prescribed actions and can apply them to any situation, dire or stable. You're not the kind of person who sees one way to build a table and runs to Home Depot as soon as it goes awry. You're the kind of person who walks back into the shop, picks up a screwdriver, a piece of scrap wood, and some glue, and sorts it out.

You're the one who gets things done.

This makes you especially useful when deadlines are tight. Which is most of the time.

▶ Working Quickly

Alan Cooper once advocated, in his book *The Inmates Are Running the Asylum* (1999), that designers be granted *months* of research and design time. In 16 years, I've never once worked on a project that offered more than a few weeks, and even that kind of liberty has been extremely rare. (Granted, Cooper spent a good chunk of time working on desktop software, back in the days of the since-reviled "waterfall" process. The web is much faster by the sheer nature of its on-demand updates.) Even now that we work in iterative design and release cycles rather than one where we hand off designs to programmers and never see them again, advance design time is simply not a luxury most companies bestow upon its teams.

It's a beautiful thing when you have three weeks to develop the UX strategy for a product and four months for development and QA testing.

Don't count on getting it.

Well, maybe if you work for a big company with multiple products and a large design team. Those situations never seem to have much urgency. But anywhere else?

At the beginning of most projects, all you hear about is how quickly they need to be finished. Clients are usually willing to pay what needs to be paid to make that happen, but it doesn't make the timeline any easier. Inside any non-giant company, you get the same pressure. They may see the value of quality design work, but they're also happy to undermine it and assume it can be done just as well in half the time. (They also frequently act as though their in-house team won't know nearly as much as an outside consultant. While this is great for people like me, I don't believe my success should come at the expense of a company's trust in the people it hires.) So research gets cut down to a few days, if you're lucky. Interaction design is two or three weeks, with some version of usability testing shoved in there somewhere. And this all happens while some developer or team is working up the back end for an *application* that doesn't even have a scope or shape yet.

Sorry, Mr. Cooper. It just ain't gonna happen the way you want.

Web projects move fast. Great design work doesn't come from having a lot of time. It comes from having a lot of *skill*. The most important of which is your ability to get things done quickly. To do that, you have to lead from the beginning.

Fortunately, there are some tricks for that.

Strategy Document

No matter how underfunded a project, always start with a *strategy document*. It can be fast. It can be minimal. It can be done in an afternoon (I've worked on a lot of projects with startups where this was certainly true).

It *can't* be overlooked.

The second you and everyone else involved *assume* agreement—the second you go without documenting the strategy—you double the time it takes to get almost anything done. You spend your time emailing and calling and explaining and defending all the reasons you should not do what the client just suggested, but rather stay focused on the already-defined objectives.

On fast projects, a strategy document always sounds like a waste of time and effort. When you skip it, you *always* find yourself remembering why you should have created one.

I've talked about this endlessly in articles and books and conference talks. I'll say it again here because nothing after this matters unless you know this part.

Strategy documents are crucial.

A lot of freelancers start off a project with a signed contract about how many pages a site will be, or some other equally insane measure of time and money. This is a serious miss. You're a designer. You can't know from a single phone call with a client what you need to design and/or build unless you're designing exactly what the client *tells* you to design. If you are, stop. Stop right now. If they knew what they needed, they would have done it themselves.

Your job as a UX professional is to figure out what needs to be designed. To figure out what the product is, what the website is about, what it will mean to its users, what purpose it will serve to all sides, what design objectives will make it better than the competitors' and serve a need or desire no one else has come up with in a unique and compelling way. And you do all this through research—by interviewing stakeholders and users, surveying the proverbial landscape of competing and complementary ideas, and all kinds of other things. This they teach you in design school. I hope.

This culminates in a strategy document.

My version lays out a vision statement, followed by a section describing the who-what-when-where-why of user circumstances, followed by a list of design criteria (a list of specific, descriptive, annotated principles to guide every design decision for the project), and ending with a list of success metrics (actual numbers you'll be able to use to measure your success later on).

Your version might look different. It might be 17 pages long. (Mine are never longer than two.) It might include a feature set. (Mine are strictly limited to high-level strategy statements. I narrow down the features in a separate file.) It might include estimated timelines. (Mine don't. Deadlines go into whichever project management app we're using. Why write anything twice?)

I keep mine short because it dramatically increases the odds that other people will read and continue to reference it. I limit it purely to strategic statements so it's divorced from hard details that make it longer and which will likely change anyway.

What matters is that it does its job. It tells everyone on the team what you're doing and why and, in some ways, how. It expresses the vision and goals.

If your deadline is harsh enough, you can do your (albeit very limited) research in the morning and write this document in the afternoon. On some bigger projects, you actually get that two or three weeks you want to do more research, and you can write pieces of the document all the while, revising as you go.

What matters most is that you *do it*.

A strategy document gives you a guidepost. An official agreement to start out with that you can use to fend off disagreement later. It settles debates.

When someone brings an idea, you pull out the strategy doc, ask whether or not the idea supports the vision and design objectives, and serves the success metrics for the project. If the idea is solid and meets all the design objectives, you've got a contender. If it doesn't, it's out. Simple as that. You say that although you can collectively consider the idea later, for now, it doesn't make the cut.

This works the vast majority of the time. Everyone knows what went into the strategy document. Everyone agreed to it. It only changes based on new information. It doesn't change just because someone decides to accommodate a new idea.

Bonus: Doing this shifts the job of cutting off a bad idea at the knees to the strategy document and away from you.

Conversely, the strategy doc tells everyone involved what to think about when making their own decisions. It gives everyone on the team a guidebook for good decisions. Write it well, communicate it well, point back to it all the time, and you'll find people bringing great ideas to the table that merely need sanity-checking. You waste no time knocking down bad ideas.

The Driver of the Bus

One more point. That really important point I mentioned a minute ago:

It puts you in a leadership position.

You were the coordinator of the strategy. You did the research. You made it clear at the start that the whole team would be biding to it throughout the project. And you are now its guardian.

This makes you the one leading the charge. You're the one who reminds people to validate new ideas through the strategy. You're the one who has the strategic authority to tell peripheral stakeholders how important it is to stick to it.

This is right where you want to be. Now all you have to do is hit your deadline. And you do that by working quickly. And there are a bunch of ways to put all those UX skills you have to work, even when the budget is tight and the deadline is tighter.

Design Time

Start by giving yourself more design time—not by adding time to the project, because you don't usually have that option, but by getting the obvious stuff out of the way.

Around 2008, Jared Spool and I noticed a trend: web teams were spending a lot of time working out the kinks of the most common elements in their projects. Things like contact forms, and error messaging, About Us sections, and lots of other boring aspects of website design were taking up valuable time, when what teams really wanted is the same as you probably want now: to work on the cool stuff. We realized that web teams, more and more all the time, needed to codify a *reuse* strategy. We looked over the design experiences I'd had, and all the research that had been done by Jared's company, User Interface Engineering, and teamed up to write a book on the subject. The book was called *Web Anatomy* (New Riders, 2009).

The basic idea was this: Although a lot of people are familiar with design patterns (common solutions to common design needs), not a lot of people are taking it beyond that. Design patterns only go so far. To really benefit from them, you can combine them into complete frameworks to create solutions for more involved problems. Design patterns may be great for very small, very specific problems, like pagination on a search results page or advanced search and the like, but they have limited value until you combine them into interaction design frameworks to address entire sections of a website. The "About Us" section of a site, for example, is pretty standard at this point. Every website *type* has its own version, but none of them need reinventing. It's the perfect candidate for a framework.

This is the obvious stuff I'm talking about.

Whenever you can on a project, free up a decent bit of design time by first whipping up a list of the basic essentials and getting them out of the way—a user profile system, for example, and the framework for the supporting content pages, like About Us and Contact. You'll often have a list of essentials like these before you even get started. Dealing with them quickly and first lets the developers get started on building something while you're busy with the rest.

Bingo. More design time.

Once you start designing, focus on the parts of the app that establish most or all of the interaction design language to be used throughout the rest of the app. This lets the developers keep going. It also makes it faster for you to transform the rest of the app's requirements, which you're about to uncover, into screen designs.

Throughout the project, keep your design deliverables light. Create as few as possible.

Faster Wireframes

First, let's look at wireframes. If you don't know:

Wireframes are early line-art versions of possible screen designs. Basically the digital versions of napkin sketches, albeit usually with more detail. They're not written in code. Their purpose is to get ideas down, possibly try them out in a round of quick usability tests to validate some ideas and hunches, and to get conversations started and agreement happening. Wireframes are a thinking tool. They're not meant to be robust, detailed design artifacts. They're meant to be quick-to-create, quick-to-revise, cheap throwaway documents. They come in a range from low-fidelity to hi-fidelity, depending on who's creating them, what software they prefer to use, and how quickly they like to work.

Their purpose best lends itself to low-fi. The quicker it is to create and change them, the better. Strategy and design cost money, and they're only a fraction of the cost of the project they contribute to. You don't want to spend a lot of money (in working hours) creating deliverables no user will ever see. Hi-res wireframes have their place—like when you need to show a big-time boss-man a high-quality version of a design you're still far away from being able to build. But high-fidelity wireframes also have drawbacks. Like when boss-man looks at a hi-res wireframe and thinks it's a nearly finished, functioning screen, and you have to explain that there's no actual code behind the grand illusion you've created and are now projecting on the conference room wall. And also when you're showing the wireframe to get feedback from other people, and everyone becomes suddenly afraid to comment because it looks like you've spent an insane amount of time on them and they don't want to ruin your day. (This happens. Seriously.)

Err on the side of low-fidelity wireframes. Then, when you show them to someone, accompany them with a good explanation of the context and what they are.

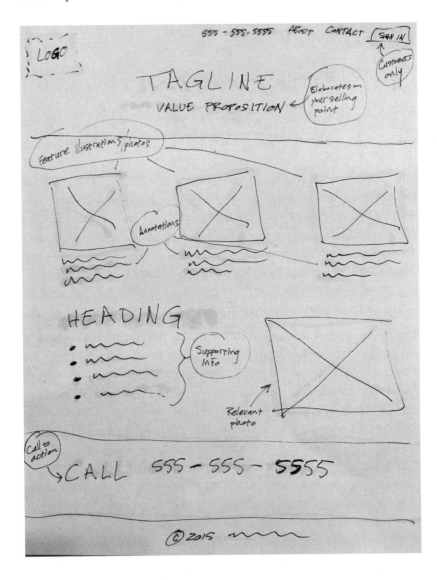

Low-fi means you'll spend less money in design hours, you'll see them sooner, and you'll get better design critiques (more on this later on in the book). The more time you spend on an idea, the more married you'll get to that idea, and the more annoyed you'll be when someone asks you to defend the idea and doesn't like your response. Better to stay unattached.

Even better is to collaborate in the first place. Talk out the objectives of the design before any pixels get pushed. Make sure the interested parties agree first on what the design needs to do—its purpose—and then focus on making it happen.

All that said, there's a big downside to both low- and high-fidelity wireframes: They suck at demonstrating function, and function is core to demonstrating the intended experience. Hence the *prototype*—an early, rough simulation of function.

Faster Prototypes

Prototypes also come in various degrees of fidelity. They are also better when they're done fast and on the cheap. Click-through prototypes, for example, are killer.

To create one, take a set of wireframes, assign click actions to elements in each screen so people can jump around between them and simulate actual task flows, then export the prototype as a PDF. Most wireframing tools offer some way to do all this, and it's by far the best way to help people make sense of wireframes and to envision exactly how the finished product might work.

Prototypes can also be made with quick, makeshift code—the advantage being that you can use real data pulled from a database and show more sophisticated functions and screen states and transitions without writing production-level code. But this takes longer. And it almost invariably ends up looking like you've put more effort into it than you intended, which can cause problems when it comes to getting feedback.

If you want to go even more minimalist than click-through PDFs, you can create a paper prototype, wherein you literally sketch different pieces and states of an interface onto sheets of paper or poster board, then walk someone through whatever task flow you want to demonstrate, whether in a team meeting or a usability test.

Speaking of.

Prototypes are great for usability tests. There's nothing cheaper than a design you can revise between testing sessions to improve throughout the day. Especially if it's made out of paper. Especially in a coffee shop. All you pay for is some coffee. And maybe a laminating machine and dry-erase markers (so you can protect it from the coffee, and reuse it all regardless). Twenty bucks and a few hours and you've got a better design and feedback from several people.

(One catch: People who are invested in completing tasks in your design because they are potentially real users of your product are generally much more willing to persevere through difficult tasks than strangers off the street who don't care one way or the other. When you can, get test participants who are truly interested in the product. The results will be more useful.)

Back in 2009, Todd Zaki Warfel wrote a great book on prototyping, appropriately named *Prototyping: A Practitioner's Guide (*Rosenfeld Media). If you want to learn more on the subject, try it out. (Full disclosure: I contributed a couple of pages to this book, so I especially dig it, but I do not receive royalties from its sale.)

Faster Usability Tests

Back to talking about usability tests.

You can do those quickly too.

When a company hits up a dedicated usability professional (as in, one who does this work full time and who these days are usually outside consultants), it's for one of two reasons. In one circumstance, it's because the people in charge have a whole bunch of work being churned out and they want to hedge their bets against a design team they don't entirely trust to be amazing every single time. Sure, they sell it to the designers by saying

"We just want to make sure we're catching all the opportunities we can to improve," but everyone knows what they mean when they say it.

When they hire one on a freelance or consulting basis, on the other hand, it's because they suspect there's something wrong with their design and a usability professional can tell them what it is. Hopefully with more depth than the people doing it in-house with maybe a tenth of their responsibilities.

Regardless, usability testing did—and still often does—go something like the following, mostly because this is how it's taught in classes and books and other places where things have to apply only in theory. (Dreams, perhaps.)

1. Usability analysts talk to stakeholders about the goals for a particular design and what the stakeholders think is cause for concern.

2. The analysts write a plan for which aspects of the design to test and how to go about it to get relevant responses.

3. They determine what kinds of people will be the most useful test participants.

    These might be avid fans of the product, people who've never even heard of it, people in their 30s with college degrees, or something else. They either maintain or buy lists of potential participants, they throw calls out on Craigslist and other sources to pull some together, or they outsource to a company whose job it is to call people and screen them for just such a purpose.

4. They schedule a few of these people to come into the office and "spend an hour telling us what you think of our designs so we can identify areas of improvement."

5. They buy gift cards for the participants, greet them at the door, feed them coffee and donuts, sit them down, and use a script they've written to carefully, deliberately explain that the participant is not being tested, the design is, and here's how it works.

6. They ask the users to perform specific tasks on the website or app or whatever it is they're testing, and to "think out loud" as they go

along so the usability pro ("test moderator" in this context) can write down the more subjective reactions to the tasks.

This almost invariably results in a few blatant lies when a user spends five minutes figuring something out and then says "It was about a 2 on the difficulty scale." Because, well, they figured it out. Eventually. Throughout this, the analysts are careful to avoid leading statements that might give the user a hint and therefore skew the results.

7. After the testing sessions are done for the day, the usability pro churns all the numbers into some percentages, breaks them down in a myriad of ways—ratings by age, education, web-savviness, all kinds of other things—and often sticks all the data into a slide deck (PowerPoint, Keynote, Google Docs) and presents it all in a meeting full of designers and developers, who then walk away appalled at their performance and with their jaws on the floor.

8. Someone hands over a very large check to pay for the whole thing.

This is the way it's often taught in school. This is how the books frequently say to do it.

Don't expect to do it this way. This painful and pricey process is why it took ten years or so for usability testing to become common. The expense alone made it hard to justify. Pressing deadlines were the other reason.

Yes, these test labs still exist. Giant companies sometimes have them. They're rare, but they're around. And using one is pretty fun. Lots of hardware and cool setups. And usability pros still run testing sessions this way. Still ask questions like that.

As they should.

But they mostly do it now while applying other methods to testing. Cheaper ones. Faster ones. Very few companies actually do anything the way it's taught in schools and books.

Again, companies rarely have the budgets and time and resources they need to get through such vigorous rigmarole. Few companies have a lab. Few have a pool of test participants to pull from anytime they need to validate an idea or prove to the higher-ups that something is wrong with a current site.

More likely, a company has a tiny bit of side cash on hand just for testing, and it's hoping you can pull off some version of it. You know, put a second set of eyes on the design. Yes, you can order up some participants from various service companies whose job it is to find and screen people according to your criteria, but this takes time, and arguably the most valuable time to run a usability test is smack dab in the middle of a heated round of design production, when interfaces are still being sketched on napkins or are merely interesting ideas. This is not the moment you want to suffer the screening and organization process of traditional usability testing. This is the moment you want to run across the street to the nearest coffee shop and come back in three hours with a design direction you're confident about.

Far more common than a test lab is some version of guerrilla testing where all you have is a few days and a smartphone. It's fast, cheap, messy, often totally disorganized. And it's fun.

And fortunately, now that it's been a bunch of years and technology (and the lack thereof) gives us ways to do it, usability pros can not only measure a design quickly, they can measure it in the right state, at the right time, and actually improve it in the process. And this makes companies very happy. They're much more willing to pay for testing when it's cheap.

First, thanks to software, built-in laptop cameras, and smartphones with high-resolution video, usability tests can be run anywhere. Coffee shops. Food trucks. Backyards. Rig up a copy of Morae (the usability testing software from Techsmith) or something else, or just set your phone on a stand, pop open your laptop, and go for it. No need for two-way mirrors and a big divided room; Morae lets people watch sessions remotely. Testing software also comes in cheaper and more nimble forms, such as Silverback by Clearleft. Whatever you use, you can piece together a highlight video of user reactions, put it in a slide deck, and play back your proof of user reactions. If a quick shock is all you need, iPhones have FaceTime. Call up the team and have everyone watch from a conference room.

I won't bog you down with how-to details. The world is full of resources through which you can learn how to do the work. What's important here is that you and your current or future boss both understand that usability testing can be done cheaply and quickly. And that this kind of rapid, sometimes jarring, incredibly useful qualitative research is what you can expect from a usability professional.

There's more.

Rather than merely test a design, you can improve it at the same time. I call it "iterative usability testing." I don't believe anyone else has named it, and we need to call it something.

1. Rather than build out an elaborate prototype, written in actual web code, use PowerPoint, Keynote, or OmniGraffle to create a click-through PDF. This is a set of wireframes with click actions assigned to all the elements you intend to be clickable in the finished product and exported as a PDF.

2. When you schedule your three to five participants, leave time between each session. Leave something like 30 minutes between the first three sessions, and 15 to 20 minutes between the others.

3. Throw the PDF onto a computer screen and have the first participant attempt to complete the tasks you're interested in testing.

4. After each session, have the designer revise the click-through prototype based on the tester's feedback, then throw a new version of the PDF on to the testing computer for the next participant. Every participant gets a new version of the design throughout the day.

Do *not* change every little thing these test participants point out. That would be ludicrous. Some of what they get tripped up on will be things you already know need work or that aren't done yet. For something small, you'll want to wait to see if the remaining participants get caught up on it as well, or if it was a fluke. Be smart about it. Change only what you really think needs changing.

This makes for a crazy day. It will exhaust you. But do this well and the last participant will have almost no issues. At the end of the day, you'll have a stronger design.

A week after the last time I walked a client's designer through how to do iterative usability testing, he said it was "exhilarating." He also said the design was now significantly better, and it took no time at all.

One note.

Some articles online may try to get you to fall in love with something called "Rapid Iterative Testing" or something fancy like that. It's basically the same as my "iterative usability testing," with one big difference: It takes longer. Instead of revising the design between individual tests, you revise after a full day of test sessions. On the first day, every participant uses the same version of the design. Then you hold a second day of testing sessions, making revisions between the two testing days. It's definitely faster than doing multiple rounds of testing over a month, but it's not nearly as quick as iterative testing over a single day.

It's a great way for consultants to make more money. It's not necessarily going to produce better results.

It also can't be definitively proven that any version is more effective than another. Usability testing isn't a rote process. For all the effort by practitioners to standardize how it's done, everyone does it a little differently. Everyone gets different results. One man's show-stopper is another man's non-issue. This doesn't mean you shouldn't hire a usability professional. Just have realistic expectations. If your design has problems (and let's face it, it will), it's *always* a good idea to lure them out so you can punch them in the face. Just know that a one-time run-through isn't the end of the process. There are always more issues waiting to be found, always more problems waiting in the darkness to mess with your potential.

If you push for a slow, expensive testing process, you may not get any testing time at all. Aim for speed. You have better things to do.

Like analyze the results. And learn from the experience.

And adapt.

4

Understanding

▶ Knowing the Psychology

▶ Applying the Psychology

▶ Talking the Psychology

After any amount of time in the web industry, you'll most certainly hear a coworker or a boss or a client refer to your users as "dumb." They talk about how we have to "dumb down" our application interfaces, design for "the lowest common denominator," and try to make our applications "idiot-proof." Once in a great while, someone says to try "the mother test," banking on the idea that if our mothers can use our applications, anyone can.

Designers say it themselves once in a while. The really terrible designers say it repeatedly.

"Well, you can only hold their hands so much."

Thing is, it's not true. Our mothers are not so stupid that we can effectively use them as the litmus test for online idiocy. Nor is anyone else. Nor is it a good idea to fall for the hype of stupid users.

A lot of designers have become convinced at various points in their careers that even the people they respect, love, and admire turn into complete morons the second they open a web browser. And designers forget that even the smartest people they know are often no smarter than anyone else when it comes to using technology.

There are *so many things* wrong with this.

First, it means the people around you have discounted the psychology involved in achieving great design. They're all walking around without any sense whatsoever that human psychology is at the heart of every single decision a user makes, and that there is no avoiding it, and that recognizing and applying this psychology to design work is literally the single most important thing a company can do to get what it wants out of a product.

Second, it means you've done the same. You haven't communicated this truth. Perhaps because you don't know it. Perhaps because you didn't know how communicating it could help you get ahead as a designer. Perhaps because you're not communicating it well enough.

Third, it means the other stakeholders will never understand just how complicated and involved it is to design something truly fantastic.

Finally, when we as designers fail to know and apply and advocate this user psychology, we encourage the rest of the world to commoditize UX work. *I'll pay you this much, and in return, I'll expect you to give me this many wireframes.* Even when you're great at it and have a stellar reputation, you are at high risk on any project that stakeholders unfamiliar to UX will look at you as, basically, a wireframe monkey.

But hey, unless we as designers understand this brutal truth, and apply it to everything we do, and preach it to every person involved, we probably won't design anything great anyway.

The blame is ours. If stakeholders want to commoditize our work, they'll have no reason not to. They'll continue to see UX professionals as the people who make the wireframes and who have somehow convinced everyone that wireframes are a good idea. And this will continue to come back and kick us in the head. Rather than educate the world around us on the complexities of designing technology to benefit its users, we'll spend our time fighting off bad ideas and complaining about how no one gets how hard it is to do it well.

Or we can turn it around.

I vote for that.

You need three elements to pull it off. You need to know the psychology, you need to apply it to your work, and you need to talk about it. A lot. Do these three and you'll be in a much stronger position to lead as a UX professional.

▶ Knowing the Psychology

First up, the psychology itself.

Here are some key things you should know about the people who use your websites and applications. Some may be obvious. Some may be surprising. Regardless, you should use this collection as a checklist to keep in mind as you design your next site. And the next one. And the one after that.

Use them to determine whether or not a feature should be added, a block of text written, or an error message shown. Use them to develop and maintain your sense of empathy toward the people on the other side of your computer screen. Use them to settle arguments and to remind those around you that they can, and should, take better care of their customers. Use them to remind yourself of the same.

Whatever you do, *use them*. (The points discussed here, by the way, hardly cover all the psychology you need to know about how people use technology. But it's a few of the necessary starting points.)

They're Smarter than You Think

I've been personally involved in hundreds of usability tests. The vast majority of the time participants have been a lot smarter than a lot of designers give them credit for. They've had college degrees. They've been professors. They've been small business owners. They've been the heads of marketing teams at large companies. Retired accountants. Teachers. All kinds of smart people doing all kinds of smart things.

They just don't care about learning your system. It doesn't matter to them. What matters to them is that *other* thing they do. The one they got a degree in. The one that pays their bills. The one *they* spend 40 hours a week doing before going home to *their* families and *their* lives and *their* problems.

It can be so easy to forget how little everyone outside the tech industry depends on personal tech the way we all do. These days, if you don't have Facebook on your iPhone, you're basically a pariah. But this way of thinking is a curse of the tech industry: We live in a bubble. We forget how easy it is to live with*out* all this stuff. And it is easy. Humanity survived a mighty long time without it. We're not going to become dependent on it overnight. Evolution doesn't work that quickly. What we can't usually get by without is some sort of way to make a living, to support families, to get to work, to make dinner. Unless technology makes itself necessary to all that, people can pretty well get by without it. Even when technology is vital to their work, they can often get by learning only the parts of it they need. So they do.

They Have Other Things to Do

Many startups seem to want to design the next major user destination. The next Facebook. One of the six sites or apps a person uses every day.

So few of them will do anything even close to that.

Even when a company is more pragmatic and aims to do something simply more engaging than all those sites that get a split-second of attention before users move on, a lot has to come together to make this happen. Contrary to what companies want to believe, the goal of most users is not to spend all their time on their website. It's to get *off* their website.

The good ones know this. The good ones have it baked into the product.

Like Google.

If Google designed to keep you on its search site, no one would use it. All the other search engines would be faster and less intrusive.

In most cases, you should focus on how to make your site or app the least time intensive. The most convenient. The most worth using because it helps users move on with their lives rather than attempt to take them over.

They Have a "Doing Mode"

You know that thing everyone believes about users not being willing to read while using an app? There's a reason for it. They're not in reading mode. They're in doing mode. We all have it. We get on a mission to complete a task, and we go blind to what could help us complete it.

Like instructive text next to a form field. That line that shows the format for how your phone number should be entered. We'll blow past that and enter it however we want. (Of course, the form should be designed to accept any version, or to automatically convert our version into the version the form needs, but that's the designer's fault.)

Or like an ad at the top of the page. Even if it's wildly interesting and perfectly relevant to something we need or want, we ignore it at all costs because it has nothing to do with what we're trying to accomplish at the moment. This is partially why ad click-through rates are so dismal, and why marketers keep inventing new ways to interrupt you with an ad you're still going to do your best to ignore, and why we all hate them for doing it.

Or like those little tips that appear when we're trying to complete a task. They're usually right there next to the thing we're staring at, and we still can't be bothered to notice them. (As a designer, this should tell you something: You'll have to design something that doesn't need an instructive tip.)

"Doing mode" has a massive benefit. It helps you ignore the distractions and obstacles keeping you from getting where you want to go. Imagine what driving would be like if you couldn't ignore the distractions. Constantly scanning billboards, reading shop-front windows, glancing at the little poster-board signs spiked into the ground at intersections. You'd never make it home alive.

It's not a flaw that people read less while in doing mode. It's a survival skill.

There's just one little downside: It means people will also often blow past your instructive text. Which means you can't rely on it as a helpful design element and you'll have to come up with a more self-teaching design.

They "Satisfice"

Another effect of having other things to do is getting through tasks just well enough.

Most people, most of the time, don't need to become experts at a particular piece of software or website or app. They need only enough skill to complete the basic tasks they use it for. Even graphic designers, who use Photoshop heavily on a daily basis, often have no idea what all its features do, or even know they exist. When people do become legitimate, heavy-use, master-level experts, it's often for a short time. It's rare.

Most of the time, people need only enough to get by. So they learn only that much. They might even learn to do something the wrong way. It doesn't matter as long as they can still get what they need done.

This is called *satisficing*. It's a term promoted by Steve Krug, whose three versions of the seminal book on web usability *Don't Make Me Think* (New Riders)—the first of which appeared way back in the '90s—is probably half the reason usability analysts exist and, in turn, a large part of why UX was able to turn into a profession. (We needed people to design stuff better in the first place.)

Satisficing is just what it sounds like. It's a portmanteau of the words "satisfy" and "sacrifice." And this, too, is a survival skill. There are not enough hours in the day, or a life, to become masters of all we touch. Most things, we just need to learn enough to get by.

They Don't Use Your Software the Way You Intend Them To

It's surprising when it happens. It's educational. It's illuminating. It's curious. It's maddening. It's a big reason that websites and apps change over time into something no one expected.

No matter how much work you put into it, the first thing people do when you put out an app with any reasonable amount of complexity is start using it in a way you didn't *anticipate*. Field labels get misinterpreted. Forms are misused. Someone needs the app to do something it doesn't do, so they *satisfice* a hack.

Sometimes it's a major drag. Sometimes it means users are doing something that could in fact be *bad* for the business. It means they're not getting what they want out of it. *You're* not getting what you want out of it. (This is why it's so beneficial to do usability testing on an early version of a design. Anything nonstandard or new runs a high risk of user confusion if you don't nail the details. Testing lets you do that.)

But then, sometimes it leads to an opportunity.

When early Twitter users wanted to reference another person, they preceded the other person's username with the @ symbol. When they wanted to reference a particular subject that reached beyond their personal timelines, they used hashtags. Twitter hadn't designed for either of these situations. Users just started doing what they wanted. Twitter followed by building in support for these two functions. Next thing you know, the whole world is talking to each other and discovering all sorts of topics they couldn't possibly have tripped over previously.

The only sad thing about this is when designers take it personally. They think it's because the users are dumb, or that the design has somehow failed. It's neither.

Take it for what it is: a chance to see a design through someone else's eye. To learn how other people interpret design elements when they don't know what you know about web design. If you take it as that, you can find amazement in it.

I mean that. Few things are more fun than watching someone interpret your design differently than you intended. Because no matter what they do, you come out of it with a lesson you won't forget. One that will make you a better designer.

The ultimate lesson to walk away with, watching this happen over and over again, is:

No matter the outcome, *you* made it happen.

When a user does the unexpected, it's because you've somehow allowed for it in your design. You may have even *encouraged* it. You just don't know how.

But this isn't bad. It means the power is in your hands. Once you see the users' unexpected behavior, you can look back at your design and make sense of it. Over time, this makes you better. It makes you able to predict a user's response.

I talk about this more in Chapter 6.

They Rely on Patterns

Pattern recognition is a major asset as a human being. Being able to spot patterns and make sense of them helps us drive, work, learn, and much more. Even when we're staring at something we've never seen before, we use patterns we learned earlier to assimilate them into our worldview. We make sense of new things by relating them to old things.

When people use technology, this happens a lot.

A *lot.*

Patterns help people learn how to work with a new app or site, how it might be set up, how long it might take. Buy a product on one department store website, and you know how most of the others work. The experiences are similar, if not nearly identical, on most commerce sites because the pattern works well for the situation and because it helps people form expectations and work through the process. If your business depends on selling products, the last thing you want users to face is a shopping task flow so completely different from any other one that they have to learn how to use your site before they can actually do anything with it. This setup carries from one site to the next because it gets the design out of the way and puts the user in a position to buy buy buy.

This is why design patterns and components (coded standards for a design element that always looks and behaves the same way) and interaction design frameworks are important. (Interaction design frameworks, as I mentioned in the previous chapter, are sets of patterns you combine to solve the larger and more rote aspects of website design, like an About Us section.)

The ability to spot and use patterns also sets the stage for the elements in a design that *stand out*. The important elements, like buttons that tell you how to Sign Up, or Send, or Save, or Publish. In a tremendous number of cases, the buttons that trigger these actions are displayed in a different color or shape or both than all the others.

When we can see patterns, we see what *breaks* those patterns.

A Million Things Are Competing for Their Attention

Right now, it's a good bet that a whole bunch of things are competing for your attention. Just like they were earlier when you were trying to finish an important email at the same time three people were stopping by your desk at work to ask about five different projects.

All the more important for a design to have an impeccable sense of what the user wants to accomplish.

A clear, deliberate, one-step-a-time process in a task flow is *vital*. Forcing people to serialize (as in, the opposite of multitask) can be hugely beneficial to their productivity with your app. If you can avoid having them jump from one app to another and check something in their user profiles just to complete a task, you should. The more the user is able to move forward, the better. It increases the odds they'll be able to finish a task without wandering off to do something else.

They See What's There

This is a big one. Because it's a straight-up communication issue, and communication is difficult. (Again, see Chapter 6, on communicating.)

Basically, there's a big difference between what *you* think you've put onto a screen and what the *user* thinks you've put onto a screen. And between you and the user, only one of your two perceptions matters.

The effect is a communication gap. You meant *this*. The user thought you meant *that*—mostly because *that* is what you actually put on the screen.

It's a classic problem. When you know a lot about the web and are designing for it, you bring a ton of information about it with you into the project. So you make some decisions along the way—not all of them, but certainly a few—that are based on your knowledge of the situation rather than the *user's* knowledge.

It's easy to do. It happens to everyone. You forget how little others know about what you take for granted by being involved in the design process. You know what that button does, and where that page sits in the site hierarchy, and what this element here means and does and why it exists. You were just explaining this to someone else on the team the other day.

Only the user doesn't have any idea why this element exists or does what it does. And the user doesn't have the benefit of having you stand over his shoulder to explain it.

You meant to write about how the sunset was a trail of fire and how the oranges and reds and purples all bled through every tree and became every reflection in every skyscraper in the jungle that is your urban hometown. What you actually wrote was, "It was amazing!"

You were supposed to design an interface that explained itself. One that told the user how it could make his day better by letting him check off this annoying chore and get it off his to-do list for a week. What you actually did was ask him to sign up without explaining the value.

You know what you *meant*. They see what you *did*. We all do it. It's a normal human failing to have a hard time being objective about the quality of our work.

Don't lose your mind over it. It's how you learn. Just remember it next time:

Users see what's actually there. Not what you *think* is there.

They Lie

This is one of the funniest things I know about people. Because it explains so much without explaining anything at all.

Generally, when you ask a person what she would say or do in a given situation, she'll come up with an answer. She may start with, "I don't know." But give her a minute and you'll get, "You know, I think I'd... "

People seem to know themselves pretty well while being asked hypothetical questions.

And yet when she's actually in that situation, she'll do something completely different.

It's not because they want to lie to you. They just can't help themselves. It takes a great deal of self-awareness to know how you'd actually act in a given situation, and few people have a *great deal* of that.

This is just one of the ways they lie. Here are a few others:

- During a usability test, as I mentioned before, testers will rate a task as having been very easy after spending five minutes figuring it out.

- In a survey, they'll say they'd use something when they wouldn't. (They just won't know that until they get their hands on the new feature.)

- In person, they'll tell you they're "web savvy," and then fumble around the computer screen for minutes on end attempting to do things you take for granted every single day. They'll type slowly. They'll click a form field to start typing when it was already selected.

- Then they'll tell you they know how to fix the issues they're having.

The list goes on and on. These are just a few that may be relevant to your design effort.

They Don't Know What's Possible

Very few tech users are also designers. Most of the time, the people who use your products have no idea what's possible when it comes to improving them. When they get tripped up by a poor design decision, they come up with an equally poor Band-Aid for it—something that may appear to fix the problem, but which really just causes other problems. When they tell you how they'd like something to work, it's usually according to their worldview—a fix that would make their problem slightly less annoying, but not one that fundamentally erases the problem's causes.

This isn't to say designers are better skilled than other people. It's to say that designers tend to know more about what factors could completely change the game. When a designer looks at an app, it's with a world of tech and design knowledge. When a user looks at an app, it's with the appropriately narrow perspective of how they use it. Hence, they have a hard time articulating what they really need or want an application to do to solve a problem for them. They don't know how to fix the problem—they just know they want it fixed. So they make suggestions.

Your job is to take them with a grain of salt. Read between the lines. See what's really causing their issue.

If You Improve Their Lives, They'll Love You

People shift to new technology or processes when those things obviously improve their lives. The "cost of switching" has to be indisputably worth the effort. If it's not, there will be no voluntary switching. Sure, some people will hop along with changes just fine, but most people want to be shown how the new way is better. How it justifies the effort of changing the way they complete tasks now. But most often, updates to an app or a website are just mandatory revisions users all have to adapt to. If those updates had never come, hardly anyone would've noticed.

If you address a real problem, however, or produce a real benefit that doesn't already exist, and you can demonstrate it, your users will love you. They'll feel included in the process. They'll feel respected. They'll enjoy your new approach to the problem.

As long as you *prove* you're making their lives better.

In the best of cases, the benefit demonstrates itself. It's obvious how the new design changes the experience for the better. In some cases, users need a good review of the changes by someone else to persuade them, or a short video on your website, or an email newsletter explaining the change.

If the benefit isn't really a benefit, no one will care what your rationale was; they'll just want to go back to the way things were. You might even find yourself actively defending your decisions.

They Come With Questions

Anytime users come across a new web app—not a content site, like a news site, but a task-based web *application*—they come with a series of questions that need to be answered right away. If these questions aren't answered, there's a solid chance they'll take off. This is because of the very human need to get oriented.

They start by glancing around the page to see what's there. They'll see the logo, the navigation, whatever's biggest on the page. They'll try to make sense of what the app *does*. Its purpose. Its promise. You can address this right away with some sort of value proposition statement that answers the question.

"We make planning your day as easy as saying Hello."

That explains the app's major purpose. It also begins to answer the user's second question: *How does it help me?*

To answer that one further, you can show a few key benefits of the app, such as a small graphic that illustrates how the user can speak into his or her phone to create a task, edit it, and mark it complete.

Next, the user wants to know how hard this app is to set up and learn. When an app is terrible, after all, no one wants to spend much time figuring that out. You can address this through a small series of graphics that show a short sign-up form, a stick figure speaking into a smartphone, and a completed to-do list, each with a few words explaining how easy it all is. For example:

"Install the app and sign up in less than 30 seconds."

"Teach it your voice (5 minutes)."

"Get going!"

When all the benefits start to look appetizing, the user wants to know how much it costs. If you have tiers or subscription pricing, or anything else that needs some qualifying, you can throw this on a Pricing page. If it's a quick and easy answer, you can put it right there next to the value proposition.

"Just $2.99 per month."

Then all you have to do is show them how to get started.

"Sign up now."

They come with questions. Your job is to deliver answers that turn them into customers. You just have to consider what questions they might ask.

Again, more on this in Chapter 6.

They Blame Themselves for Mistakes When They Should Blame You

There is an *acceptable* user experience. One everyone involved in the project would be all right calling a success. It's the one where a lack of complaints means everything is dandy. It happens when users are capable *enough* of getting through the app. Most of the time, anyway. Where adoption and usage rates are decent *enough*.

It happens when loads of opportunities to improve a design still exist, but no one knows this because users aren't complaining.

It's the kind of experience that turns ugly only when you pay close attention—when you watch people use your site or app and hear what they say out loud. Because that's when you find out why they're not complaining.

When designers have problems with an interface, they blame its designers. When people have problems, they blame themselves. They think they're not smart enough to use the app. They say they didn't get enough sleep to understand it. They say it's too advanced for them.

Is this a good user experience? No. It's a bad user experience hidden by the fact that everyone having it is blaming the wrong person.

A lack of complaints doesn't mean there aren't any. It means you may not be hearing them.

Their "Experience" Is Based on Far More than Your Website

No matter how thorough you are in researching and designing a product, it's pretty unlikely you're going to do something that will change a person's life. You probably won't even improve a person's day.

UX is the net sum of all the interactions and impressions and feelings a person has with a website, digital product, or service. Their impressions of your design are affected by a lot more than just your design. They're affected by the company's reputation, if they know what it is. They're affected by what other people have said about the company or product, whether negative, positive, or undecided. They're affected by what it looks like, and how they've felt in the past about other things that looked similar to it. They're affected by how they feel that day and how open they are to this new product at the moment they encounter it. They're affected by how well they can learn it, what they might get out of it, how frustrated they've been by other products that have failed to do what they promised. You name it; it has an effect on a user's experience.

▶ Applying the Psychology

An extraordinary amount of brain stuff is working with and against you as a designer.

This fact probably explains why it's always so difficult for other people to understand why no one ever nails a design on the first try, and why it's never really "done." It also probably explains why you have such trouble in the attempt to nail it.

Good.

If I've made this clear, I've made my point. It's time for more designers to dig deep into psychology and apply it to design work.

Over the years, it's become more and more obvious to me how much it affects every decision a user makes. How much is at play when a user approaches a site, tries to make sense of it, decides whether or not it has value to them, or attempts to use it? Do all the user research you want. Until you embrace the effects of psychology on a user's experience and design for it, you'll get nowhere.

And yet once again, the articles and books and courses on design ignore this. It's incredibly rare to see one that connects the dots between psychology and design best practices.

So let me try.

Imagine you're designing a web application that aims to help people who work on contract to create and manage invoices. Basically, the site will be task-based, and will require users to sign up to gain access to their own user home page, which gives them ways to create a new invoice, send one, see the payment status of open invoices, and otherwise manage them (delete, resend, edit, comment, send reminders, and so on). Somehow, you want to make it different and better than all the other sites doing the same thing. Different is a selling point. It means instead of competing one-for-one, you're competing by standing out. It's Business 101: You win by being different.

Take a look around at a few sites that with similar structures—project management sites, to-do list sites, accounting sites, whatever—and you'll see a few commonalities. As I mentioned in the "They Come With Questions" section, each site will make a pitch on the home page. Each one will offer a way to sign up through a big button with a strong call to action (CTA). Each one will attempt to explain the benefits of using *this* app over *that* *other* one. Each one will tell you about its pricing plans. Just by looking around at a few sites, you can see that these things seem to be considered best practice, and that you should probably do them as well. Years of usability tests have told the designer world that these elements are effective at convincing users to sign up.

Rarely does anyone explain why. You can find a million articles about what makes an effective home page for a subscription web app, but have you ever seen one that explains the rationale behind the decisions?

Home page design used to be completely erratic and nonsensical. Bad pages were far more common than good ones. Over time, the good ones have won out. These days, for subscriptions sites like this invoicing app, it's extremely common for home pages to feature all the elements I've just described, used in the same way, frequently laid out in the same order.

Is it because everyone's thinking about the psychology and coming to the same conclusions?

No. They're mostly just copying each other. I almost never come across a designer who points to psychology as the reason for anything. Mostly, it's just that they've read the articles and followed them to the letter. They've copied the other sites. They did the same thing. So much for being different.

Here's the thing.

Understanding the psychology *behind* the design is the only way to design for it differently than everyone else does.

You know why these elements are effective. It's not because that's what everyone else does. It's because people come to a website with questions, and these elements answer those questions.

Are they the *only* way to answer these questions? No. Not even close.

And here comes the obligatory Apple reference.

Remember when Apple released the iPhone? Remember the television commercials? They weren't about lifestyle. They didn't show a montage of cool twenty-somethings climbing mountains and dancing at clubs and hanging out by the pool, enjoying the insta-connectivity of their phones, which blend seamlessly into their lives. That first round of commercials showed a hand. A hand holding an iPhone. A thumb reaching over the screen and tapping things. A thumb tapping the screen, a screen responding. A thumb pulling up a map. A thumb taking a photo. A thumb sending a photo.

In 30-second bursts of televised brilliance, Apple was teaching people how to use the phone. And answering all kinds of questions in the process.

How do I use this thing? What does it do? Does it take pictures? What can I do with the photo afterwards? Oh, it has a map *application*? Is it a major pain in the neck to use like it is on my current phone?

Apple didn't say the iPhone would make you young again. It wouldn't make you a better tennis player. Or teach you how to cook. It didn't show a list of benefits. It showed a series of uses, all of which you could then inject your benefit into. *When it's so easy to use the web on this phone, maybe you could use it to settle bar bets on the fly.*

Apple didn't answer the potential user's questions in the same way everyone else does. It dug into the psychology and came up with a new way to do it. It was *different* before it was even a real thing that people could hold in their hands. The company created significant competition before you could even buy the product.

As a major bonus, these commercials ensured that buyers knew how to use the phone on the very first day. This was the first touchscreen phone to exist in all of human history, and yet most people could pick it up and start using it on the first try. Apple completely nullified the learning curve.

Imagine taking the same approach with your invoicing app—answering those questions without using the same tricks. Putting out something different enough and great enough to make other companies compete with it rather than the other way around.

Psychology is what gets you there.

There isn't just one way to answer a user's questions. There isn't just one way to make a task flow clear, because people are distracted by other things competing for their attention. There isn't just one way to get people excited about your app, to help them enjoy using it.

The ways you come up with will entirely depend on your situation, your app, your users, your goals. But no matter what approaches you take, psychology is your best tool. The more you understand it, the better you'll be able to apply it to do something truly unique, truly great, and truly exciting.

I have been saying these things for years now. I've cited psychological studies and case studies and personal studies on every project I've worked on for a decade. And still, so few designers take this subject seriously enough.

Be one of them. Besides the insights it will give you, the strategic abilities you could never achieve otherwise, an ongoing pursuit of psychological understanding will make you stand out in a massive sea of designers. You will be the one designer in the crowd who can explain user behavior. Who can learn from it. Who can apply those lessons to do great design work.

▶ Talking the Psychology

Let's recap for a second.

The root of design is psychology. Anything else is art or decoration or something else. A design is a plan, and a plan requires an intended outcome. For design to succeed, human psychology has to be at the center of it. No user can ever have the kind of feeling you hope they'll have about your product unless you consider how they'll approach it, get through it, and talk about it later. Some elements will be used to convince them of the value of the product. Others will encourage users to take specific actions. Others will surprise them, placate them, make them laugh, tick them off. Whatever the intent, the approach should be applied to all design decisions you make.

This much you know.

But even if you knew all that before reading this chapter and those before it, it's easy to forget that other people don't think about this like you do. They don't know that the root of design is psychology.

So tell them.

Please, please, please tell them.

You have so many reasons to tell them. Communicating the psychology behind your design decisions has several very important effects on your ability to lead as a designer.

First, it helps other stakeholders unfold the justifications for design decisions, which helps them trust you. It shows them the complexity of human behavior and how design needs to work with it rather than against it by designing from opinion rather than insight. It also communicates to them that you've taken a considered, insightful approach to solving the problems they brought to you.

Second, it lets them question decisions with at least partly the same arsenal of knowledge you used to make them. This is vital. No designer can make great decisions all the time, every time. Designers need feedback. They need to be asked questions just as much as they need to answer their own. The questions other people ask can help you identify potential issues on your thinking. Consider angles you haven't considered. Develop new ideas. Improve the ones you've already had. When others know the psychology of design as well, they can ask you the questions you haven't yet answered.

Talking about the psychology involved in design also helps you think through your decisions yourself. It's easy to convince yourself of something in the silence of your own mind. When you say it out loud, explanations form that couldn't have before. Out loud, out in the sunlight, your justifications change into something else. They change into rhetoric. And rhetoric has the benefit of being bidirectional. Arguments need to be made out loud where they can be considered and shifted and changed into something better.

When you bring your recommendations to the rest of the team, take the time to explain how those decisions were made. Never, and I mean *never*, hand over a set of wireframes or a prototype without explanation. Don't explain how to use the pseudo-interface you've designed—that would be cheating. Rather, explain the psychology that this version addresses. Explain why it can be beneficial to increase the number of steps in a task flow (hint: when you need for users to carefully enter uncommon information, slowing them down can help ensure they do so). Explain why a simple registration form that only asks for a few common pieces of information shouldn't be split into four screens (hint: because quicker forms in these cases tend to convert at a higher rate). Explain why a page about an in-home service your client's company provides should end with a call-to-action button, like "Schedule A Service" (hint: because without it, the page is a dead end, and dead ends are bad).

I once worked on a project that called for interviewing a saleswoman for an insurance company a few times. We talked a lot about how she vets potential customers—how she determines their needs and their budgets and balances those things out to guide the person toward a solution that works and that the person is more likely to buy. Toward the end of one of those calls, I was explaining a few of my recommendations for the insurance application form we were working to revise, and why each step should be handled that way. After a few minutes, she took a loud breath as though she'd been listening intently, and said, "There's so much psychology involved!" To which I replied, "You're in Sales. Design is just like that."

And it is. You're figuring out what makes customers tick just like salespeople do. If you can't do this well, go find a salesperson to learn from. Go find a psychologist. Go find books about decision making and persuasion and the nature of desire and buyer's remorse and intrinsic motivation and anything else you can dig up about how people think, all of which will help you understand why they do the things they do. Find blogs. Find conferences. (I'm not going to prescribe a bunch to you here, because frankly, the *hunt* for these things makes the lessons stick better, and any source I could reference is just as likely to be gone by the time you read this. Start Googling. It'll change your life.)

UX is a lot more than checkboxes and radio buttons. UX is psychology applied to design. For so many reasons, it's high time everyone else finds that out too.

5

Questioning

I have a tattoo on my neck. At first glance, most people think it's a phoenix. This is what you see if you focus only on the curving black shape inked there. The positive space. The *obvious* space. The image you can't help but see because everything points to it.

Then there's the negative space.

If you let your mind complete the outside circle and then focus on the negative space, you see something else.

See it?

Now, why on Earth would I tattoo a question mark on my neck? Especially that one?

It's because *questioning* is the fundamental tenet of my lifetime. It's the driver behind nearly everything I have said and done in my career. It's the most important thing I have to teach, and the most important thing you can learn. And my tattoo's design in particular forces people to look at it differently, which is what questioning is all about.

Questioning gives you new perspective. It forces you to see past the obvious. To see past false truths and false gospels and false idols.

When designers are capable of great work, it's invariably because they're adept at seeing past the obvious. They challenge what they see around them. They ask questions. They work to find the *better* on the other side of the *now*.

Questioning is one of the most effective actions you can take to lead a design effort rather than become the victim of its constraints. You can ask questions to form the big picture. To uncover the details your client left out of the project overview. To find out what your users really need. To dig up the *real* problem you're trying to solve—beyond the one the stakeholders brought to you.

You can ask questions to help people realize the issues in their plans. You can cast doubt on standards and "best practices." You can uncover what you didn't know, and learn as a result.

You can make people realize how much deeper the question goes.

▶ Questioning Everything

Over the years, some very smart people have questioned our assumptions as designers and discovered that we may have taken some truths for granted. I have two great examples: the belief that simplicity is a goal of good design, and that usability testing is an effective way to prioritize problems in existing designs.

People have spent years telling us these notions are true. Experts have advocated them, and designers everywhere internalized them and then passed them on to their clients and coworkers. A lot of people have made a lot of money preaching these ideas.

But those people who told us these things are true, were they right? And if they were right, is there only one version of right? Is the truth as they see it the whole truth?

Nope.

Accepting anything as the whole truth prevents you from finding the whole truth. It doesn't help you do better. It *prevents* you from doing better, because this is conventional thinking, and conventional thinking gets in the way of progress. Standards get in the way of finding the best solutions. Facts get in the way of truth. And the truth as you see it, very often, is incomplete. Much of what you accept as truth is in fact an obstacle to it.

Conventional thinking holds you back. It prevents you from becoming a better designer. It prevents you from doing the best you can for your users. It prevents you from moving your profession forward.

Questioning what you know helps you find better answers. And the most crucial time to ask questions is when you think you already *know* the answers.

To demonstrate this, consider the examples I just raised.

Questioning Ideas

Don Norman, author of many books, including *The Design of Everyday Things* (first published in 1988, Basic Books), was skeptical of the idea that everything in the world should be "dead simple." He said in a talk that he likes to "question the obvious," and simplicity is definitely an obvious design goal. And what he realized was surprising to many people.

He saw that much of what we consider simple is in fact not that simple. The Apple homepage has historically been a great example of this. For several years, the page featured just a couple of gigantic entry points, such as a large image promoting the next version of the operating system, or the new iPhone or iPad or Apple Watch, or something else.

But this homepage has never been as simple as it seems. In fact, it has actually served as the entry point for a couple of dozen different parts of the Apple website. As of this writing, the Apple homepage has 25 different links. It has links to different sections, links to customer service and reseller information, press releases, and a lot more. Twenty-five! But on any given day, Apple really wants you to think about just one. One thing Apple believes most people want to know about most. So they make it the main feature of the page.

Don Norman cites the example of a washing machine that was supposedly simpler than others but had more controls. It turns out that people often don't buy what appears simple because they believe it does less. People make purchasing decisions, in part, based on feature lists. They buy what has more features. We all do. As Don says, "Features win over simplicity, even when people realize that it is accompanied by more complexity."

By questioning the notion of simplicity as a design goal, Don Norman shows us that we're focusing on the wrong goal.

Apple didn't make the page simple. They made it clear. The washing machine didn't have fewer features; it had a better design. Despite all the hype that we must make things dead simple and dumb them down, simplicity is not the goal—clarity is.

Questioning Standards

In the late '90s, Rolf Molich (co-inventor, with Jakob Nielsen, of the heuristic evaluation method) started the Comparative Usability Evaluation (CUE) series to establish a set of best practices for usability tests. Several times over, he hired multiple teams to evaluate a single design and report their results. And what he found was also surprising.

When different teams look at the same design, they see incredibly different things. Nine usability teams evaluated Hotmail.com, and of the several hundred problems they discovered, only a small percentage were noted by more than half the teams. Worse, most of what were called "serious" or "critical" problems were reported only one time.

He saw a similar result when he hired 17 teams to evaluate a hotel reservation system.

Usability testing is great for a lot of things. It's great for validating new design ideas. It's great for feeding your instincts. You have no better way to learn how people work than to watch them work. It's great for helping people on this side of the screen understand the people on the other side.

What is it not great for? It's not great for finding the problems in an existing design to determine what you should try to fix. It's terrible for that. Because no single team will find the same issues as another team.

But Was It a Bad Test?

Because I've posited the argument that usability testing is not great at finding a problem with an existing design before, I know some of you will say this happened because those old usability tests were performed badly. But really? All 17 teams who tested the hotel reservation system did their tests badly? Rolf Molich, of all people, couldn't find better teams? Testing methods are no more consistent today than they were back then. They *all* depend on human beings writing good test plans, moderating the sessions well, and creating the right environment and testing conditions. Forcing consistency isn't simple, even when testing the same designs.

If you're using usability tests to uncover problems in your existing designs, you can spend a lot less time and money by having a lone reviewer do it instead, because what a lone reviewer finds will be no better or worse than what you find in an expensive round of usability tests. But this doesn't matter. When you're doing tests for this purpose, your goal isn't usually to prove exactly what's wrong, but merely that something *is* wrong, so you can make your case to the stakeholders for new design efforts. The time you most need to know exactly *what's* wrong with a design is before you build it. It's your first chance to get it right, and if you do, you'll never have the big problems you'll have later on by forgoing testing.

Hence, use usability testing to test *new* ideas, not old ones. Use it to validate the atypical design ideas. The new widget you've come up with that hasn't been done before. Use it to test the core task flows of your application before you spend all that cash building them.

By questioning how usability testing is done, Rolf Molich has shown how and when you can put this valuable tool to its best use.

Questioning People

When it comes to challenging convention, people are among the toughest walls to break through. It's easy to question a standard or a best practice, because they don't have any faces behind them. Standards and best practices have existed for a while and can't really be pinned on anyone in particular anymore. Sitting at a conference room table face to face with the person who needs to be questioned is a whole different story. And it's a situation *every* designer will face. Many times.

A couple of years ago, I consulted on a few projects for one of those crazy large companies that everyone's heard about and whose products everyone uses. At that time, the US government was about to enact a law that would affect many millions of people. This company—let's call them Big Fish Inc.—was worried about how the new law would affect their business, speculating it could cause several hundred thousand of its users to go to a competing company, since several of Big Fish's competitors were building products to help people deal with the effects of the new law. Big Fish, in other words, was way behind.

So they kicked into gear. They formed a team. The company's beloved former CEO committed to coming out of retirement for a couple of weeks to help guide the process. They started sketching out ideas.

The plan had a few problems. For starters, the team was composed of middle managers, product managers, and, well, *managers*. It included a single graphic designer who was splitting his time between this project and another. The team's process evidently started *without* a kickoff meeting in which everyone could get a plan together and move in unison. And since the former CEO was coming in the next week for the first time and most of the managers were new, awestruck by him, and aiming to impress, they wanted—right away—to roll out something worth showing up to see. Granted, they had a three-week deadline in the first place, but they were going to try to make a big dent in that by getting something done fast, before the CEO even walked into the room.

The CEO showed up on a Tuesday. The managerial army started gathering in the project's war room 45 minutes early to get organized.

They pulled printed sheets of hi-res design work from their folders and tore off small pieces of tape and began leaving a trail of step-by-step screen designs on every wall in the room, including the hallway leading into it. This took some effort; because these walls, most of which were covered in whiteboard paint, were already plastered with sticky notes, notes written in dry-erase marker, arrows, boxes, bullet point lists, and exclamation points, many of which needed to be moved and rearranged to make room for the Trail of Comps, sponsored by Adobe Photoshop. (That's not a real thing.)

I rolled in 15 minutes early to look around, introduce myself, and catch up on the sticky-note plans. High on one wall was a large piece of butcher paper, on which was written something like: "VISION: To offer the fastest, clearest, best customer experience in the industry."

A statement that, you know, could've applied to pretty much anything.

The former CEO's assistant came in and said he'd be there in a few minutes. The group spent most of that few minutes anxiously rechecking things. When the CEO walked into the room, they all quickly sat down.

Silence.

Introductions all around, mild laughter at even remotely funny things to come out of the CEO's mouth, and then finally, the tour around the room.

The idea was that Big Fish Inc. would offer the public—not just their users, but anyone—a way to get all the answers they'd ever need about the big new national law. It would start with a Welcome screen. You'd progress through a series of overview-type bits of information, then gradually into more specifics. Wizard-style. Click click click done. And now, please sign in to your account so we can up-sell you to a higher-tier plan and you can get the most out of your account.

The CEO reacted to that last part first. "I think it's important we don't use this as an advertising opportunity. Let's be selfless. Let's just deliver value and ask for nothing in return."

It was noble enough. Nods all around the room. No one had a counter-argument.

Next, the CEO stood, picked up a dry-erase marker from a shelf along one of the walls, removed its cap, and started asking questions. Like a *boss*.

What is our goal? What do these users need to know about how this law will affect them? What will be their biggest concern? How can we meet them there with big value?

Answers flew around the room, all unconvincingly in perfect support of the images shown along the Trail of Comps. Rather than answer the questions, in other words, the managerial collective defended their completed work. And bit by bit, the CEO whittled away at their confidence in any one of the decisions they'd made prior to arriving to work that day. When it came right down to it, they didn't have any great answers for why they'd done what they'd done. This was about the time the CEO chopped their heads off.

"Is this really what people need?"

I hadn't spoken yet except to introduce myself. But I'd be lying if I said I hadn't been grinning almost the entire time the CEO made his way around the room, demolishing one chunk of false reasoning after another. And by this time, to that question, I only had one word to chime in with.

"No."

He pointed at me with the dry-erase marker and prodded for more.

"This is a huge law," I said. "Every adult in America knows about it. They all wonder about it. It's going to be all over the news, all over *everything*. The answers to these questions are going to be on *Huffington Post*, CNN, the *New York Times*, the evening news, the local news. You name it. Pretty much none of them will need to come to this website to answer these questions, and since this company is most known for something else, few of them would even think to look here."

The company may have been a big fish, but they were jumping into a *gigantic* pond with a whole lot of other big fish already in it. This entire approach was a joke, with no thought behind it at all.

The effort hadn't started with questions. No one had asked any along the way. The managerial collective was just trying to get something going. To impress the CEO. To show they could snap to it and earn their keep and lead the charge and crank out good, smart work. Only it wasn't good. It wasn't smart.

Smart work starts with smart questions.

And the CEO was the only one asking any. He was the only one more concerned with good work than with proving himself. He had nothing to prove. He was the former CEO. He'd retired rich and beloved nearly two years earlier.

Because he knew how to ask questions.

There's just one problem with my Big Fish Inc. story. I learned about it the day after the meeting. I haven't forgotten it. It's one you should know, too, lest you suffer the same fate.

Roughly a week or so before I was invited into the project, someone had formed that team of managers. Someone had appointed one person in particular to be the head of that team of managers. Let's call him Stew. And that person, in turn, had seen in this project a chance to make a great impression. To set himself apart from the list of middle managers and do something that would be seen as impressive to the former and beloved CEO. It was a chance to put a proverbial feather in his cap.

Stew charged in. He got his team going quickly and with unwavering direction. Those designs taped up all over the walls came together in mere days. If this went over, he'd be seen as the guy who could master a tough situation in no time flat. A real leader, he'd be.

When the CEO walked in with his dry-erase marker, the air in that leader's lungs got sucked right out of the room. Stew's work was shredded. Picked apart like that weird meat attached to the joints of a roasted chicken. There wasn't much left of him by the time the meeting ended.

At that point, he had a few options. He could take a deep breath, realize where he'd gone wrong, and set about putting together a new strategy and turning his second chance at leadership into one where he was better and wiser. The other option was to blame someone.

He chose the latter.

He couldn't blame the CEO, though. Everyone loved the CEO. The CEO knew how to get things done. Blaming the CEO would get him exactly nowhere.

Stew could, however, blame the people around him. Namely, that new guy who walked into the room and disputed the very core of Stew's ideas and direction with a single word: No.

Stew, being a middle manager and the guy in charge of this particular project, decided then and there that I would go nowhere near another one of his projects ever again. I was off that project. And since he was chummy with other middle managers, it was going to be difficult from now on to get buy-in for using me on other projects in the company.

I finished out the project I was already shoulder-deep into, packed up my laptop, flew home, and stopped taking two-day trips to Big Fish Inc. I haven't worked with them since.

No matter what I thought of Stew's project leadership chops, or his ego, or his readiness to blame other people rather than himself, I forgot something in the process of calling him out: He'd put work into that project. It was bad work, but it was work. He'd spent time, and energy, and nights, and probably a weekend on it. And he wasn't about to handle it gracefully when someone tore it up while pacing the conference room floor. Even if it wasn't actually the guy he blamed.

All I really did was back up the CEO, who I thought was right. But the CEO did his crushing with finesse. I did it with a jackhammer.

And that's the lesson to learn here.

It's not that you shouldn't question people. It's that it takes some serious skill to do it well. And forgoing that skill could take away your shot at being involved in the outcome at all.

This was not my usual tactic. As a UX strategy consultant, *I'm* usually the one pacing the floor with a dry-erase marker and sorting out the strategy. I usually do this by asking a lot of questions, especially when I think something is right or wrong. Questions help the group or person come to conclusions on their own. And if there's information I don't yet know, questions help me find that out before marrying myself to that idea that someone's wrong.

For some reason, in this conference room, in this situation, I bailed on finesse. And I was forced to remember something for all time:

Read the room.

Find out who's who. Who's in charge, who did what, who made which decision. Know their names. Take mental notes about their reactions and their investments and their beliefs. *Know them.*

If you're going to question people, you need to know in advance what will work. You can think they're wrong. You can think they messed up. You can think they're the best designer you've ever met. If you're going to question them, you need to consider how to get the best outcome for both of you. Because if you're questioning someone, it's probably because they're on the same project you are, and love it or hate it, you're going to get there *together.*

Toes and egos are delicate things. You can't just go around stepping on them.

Learn how to read the room. When you see people uncomfortably shifting in their chairs, step lightly. Even if now's your only shot to shift the direction of momentum before all hell breaks loose, it has to be done with an eye for considering the other people at the conference table.

It takes patience. It takes empathy. It takes understanding. For the most part, people want to do good work. When they don't, it's not usually for a lack of trying. It's because they were missing key information that could've changed everything. It's because they panicked and rushed into it. It's because they desperately wanted to impress someone and were nervous. It's because they were in over their heads.

Every single cause of bad work has a good intention behind it. Before you question a person's work, question where it came from.

When you have no time, no budget, and even less patience for bad decisions, it can feel like an impossible task to take a deep breath and consider how to move forward in a way that puts everyone at their best. But—and I can't stress this enough—taking that breath is the *only* way to get great work out of a bad situation.

Being a UX leader isn't a part-time job. Leaders lead all the time. When they don't, they're seen as erratic and unreliable, not to be trusted. If you want to make great things happen, *right now* is always your best chance.

This is not a lesson I enjoyed learning. I'm glad I got the chance to learn it.

Questioning Your Own Work

Here's another tough lesson to learn (unless someone tells you about it, like I'm about to): how to question your own work.

As designers, we all want to believe we have good ideas all the time. Good taste. That we make good decisions. But any one of us is probably just as prone to screwing things up as anyone else. Even the most experienced among us have blind spots. (I learned the other day that I have a tendency to start sentences with the word "there," which doesn't add any real meaning to a sentence. And I've been at least a part-time professional writer for over a decade.)

There are some ways around this. (See what I did there?)

Let's say you're doing a round of usability tests on a new design you've whipped up. You've done tests like this before. You know how they go and how to do them. Before you get too caught up, ask yourself: *Do I really think I can be objective during a usability test when the victim is my own design?*

It's easy to believe you can. Odds are you can't.

Turn it over. Take a half hour to explain to someone else on your team what your goals are for the design, what you're concerned about, what circumstances would be true when a person comes across this feature or task flow, and let *that* person handle the testing. Basically: Never test your own designs. You'll be too prone to asking questions that lead the user toward the right conclusion. You're too prone to find yourself explaining to a user what you meant and not what you did.

No real user of your design work will have the benefit of you standing over their shoulder. Your design has to work on its own. For you to find out how well it can do that, it must be tested by someone more objective than you are.

The other way is data.

Once your design is out in the wild getting eaten up by people who like your product, you can watch the numbers. Stick tracking code on everything you put out into the world so you can see how it performs. Find out whether or not people are getting through that task flow. Find out at what rate they're completing registrations and buying products and making their way through the entire shopping cart. Find out where they get stuck. Where they submit the wrong information. What they share. Track it all. Data does its job independently of your beliefs, your intentions, and your skill. If you want to question your own work, follow the numbers.

One note, and I'll illustrate it with a story.

The first time I turned in a book chapter, it was to my first real editor, who worked for my first real publisher. I had always believed prior to this that I was a pretty decent writer. I was, after all, the guy everyone went to in school to proofread their work. When I got the chapter back from my editor, however, it was *dripping* in (digital) red ink. Nearly every single line had been changed in one way or another. Sentences had been rearranged. Comments had been added to ask about my intention or to point out how I'd started a topic and then abandoned it. Words had been replaced.

I was livid. For hours, all I could think or talk about was how offended I was that this guy thought my writing needed so much work. It was a few hours before the anxiety died down. That's what anxiety does. Always. It dies down. And when it does, you see things differently.

I looked over the chapter again. I accepted a few small edits. Punctuation issues. Spelling mistakes I hadn't noticed. Sure, he was right about those.

Then I looked over a few questions he'd added in the comments and answered them. Oh, wait. I see what he means here. Well, actually, I see how that could be confusing. Interesting question here. Good catch there.

Huh.

By noon the next day, he had me. It occurred to me that I'd never really been edited before. Not like this. Not for a book people were going to pick up off a shelf, and pay for, and take home, and *read*. This was a different experience indeed.

I was going to learn a lot from this guy.

And I did.

And later, when I had another editor, I learned more. And that kept happening for a long time. It still happens. Now, I *crave* good editing. It makes me better.

If you haven't watched the numbers on your own design work before, you're going to hate it for a while. You're going to wonder how people could so *extremely* misinterpret your design. This will be especially true when you're new to design work.

Give it some time. Once your nerves settle and you sleep on it, you're going to see value in that data.

Let the data question you. It *will* make you a better designer.

▶ Pushing the Profession Forward

These stories and methods add up to something important.

They show that there's always a chance to learn and uncover and rethink and redefine what we all think we know and what eventually kicks us in the shins and runs away laughing. We always have a chance to unlearn the world and let it re-teach us.

We should seize it.

Taking on the world by questioning everything about it isn't a chore. It's not just more stuff you have to do now. It's a privilege. And it's endlessly rewarding. It's how we got to walk on the moon. It's how we got to come back home safely. To get anywhere, to make progress, we have to unlearn our assumptions and dig for stronger knowledge.

We have to refuse to accept conventional wisdom and see it for what it is: conventional. Old. Boring. Stagnant.

Tipping Sacred Cows

The crackerjacks of our profession—Rolf Molich, Don Norman, Stephanie Troeth, Christina Wodtke, Jared Spool—they've all questioned what designers had previously accepted as fact and discovered that there is more to these so-called facts than meets the eye. They've walked up to the sacred cows of our profession, and they've tipped them over.

This is the kind of thinking that makes us better designers. This is the kind of thinking that improves our users' lives. This is the kind of thinking that *pushes our profession forward*.

In the end, it doesn't matter what anyone says about how to become a better designer, or what it really means to be a UX professional, or what techniques you should and shouldn't use. It matters that you ask those questions yourself and keep pushing what you do beyond where you thought it could go.

Brilliant insights are not the result of conventional thinking. Mind-blowing work is not the result of standardized, rote processes. You will never do the best work of your life by doing exactly what everyone else is doing.

What will make you better? Exactly what made Rolf, Don, Stephanie, Christina, Jared, and many more people better:

Questions.

You improve yourself, your work, your clients, and your profession not by accepting what you know but by questioning what you know.

When we question the answers we have been given, we discover the answers we have not.

Firing Away

For the good of your profession, your work, your clients, and most of all, your users:

- Ask why. Ask for an explanation. A justification. Ask this over and over and over until no answers are left to uncover.

- Ask for evidence.

- Ask if there's a better way.

Question the people who get up on conference stages. Ask them to justify what they say—to demonstrate that their ideas are good. Don't do this because you want them to fail. Do this because you want them to succeed.

At work, question your designs. Question the decisions made before. Question the decisions being made now. When something is considered standard, ask if it's really the best solution. Ask if there's a better way. Not all designs become standard by being better. Many become standard by being most noticeable. When clients say they need to add features, don't ask how—ask why. The next time someone tells you the best way to do your job, ask if there's an even better way.

Now is always a good time to look into the eye of a sacred cow and ask it what it's doing there. Find your sacred cows, and tip them over.

Always Ask the Question

Besides all that, there's another compelling reason to ask questions.

One of the more common things I've been asked over the years is how I got into the position I'm in—the one where I get to write books and articles and speak at conferences and all that. In my attempts to answer, I've told a lot of stories. They all seemed to have the same theme. Eventually, I realized what it was.

Always ask the question.

A bunch of years ago, I asked a guy I knew from a discussion list how he got into writing tech books. He answered. Another time, I asked the editor of an online magazine how I might be able to contribute to its weekly arsenal of new content about web design. She answered. Soon after that, I asked a conference organizer how I could become a speaker. That person answered.

I kept going. It seemed to be working. The more I asked, the easier it became. The more I asked, the more people said yes. The more I asked, the more I realized there's no mystery to any of this. All those things people think are impossible? Or that happened because of some big break? Or because that guy over there is really lucky? It's all crap. All you have to do is ask questions.

You know that feeling you get when people ask you about your favorite subject? When they lean in and get all attentive and conversational? When they're as excited and interested in your favorite subject as you are?

Yeah. That's all there is to it. Other people love it as much as you do.

When you express a sincere interest in something another person cares about, that person will generally do backflips to tell you about it. When you say you want to be involved, that person will get you involved. When you bring value to the thing *they* care about, that person will drag you in and never let go.

Asking that first simple question got me a book deal. (Two, actually; I had to choose between them.) And the chance to write a ton of articles on my favorite subjects. And better jobs. And better projects. And a higher income. And a better life all around than I'd ever expected when I got into this funny thing called "web design" because it was cool and interesting and looked like fun.

And that's my point.

Questioning isn't just for challenging ideas. It's for gaining benefits. If you're curious, ask. If you're unsure, ask. If you want to know more, ask. If you want in, ask.

Ask, ask, ask.

There is simply no end to what you can discover, gain, and do as a result of simply asking questions. When you think you've heard the answers, ask more.

Question the status quo. Question the standards. The people you work with. The experts. Your own designs. Your client's motivations. How to get into things. How to help. Decisions. Rules. Processes. Ask the questions, then question the answers. Question everything.

Always ask the question.

I value this idea so much, I tattooed it on my neck.

6

Communicating

Because I'm over 40 and in a seriously crotchety phase, I recently tapped on a pane of glass in my living room window to shoo off the pigeons sitting on the roof, who had been driving me crazy for days. Because I live in a historic house with single-pane windows that are about a hundred years old, my hand went right through it.

This did not help make the pigeons more endearing. But no big deal. Cardboard, tape, done. At least it's covered.

I called the first window repair company I could Google. I used the form on their website to tell them exactly what I needed.

> "I need a pane of glass replaced. It's 9" x 8.5". It's a single piece of glass that goes into a multi-paned window frame made of wood. The window is in the living room. It faces the driveway. It's a one-story historic house. Please tell me how much that might cost and when you could come out to replace it."

I've been doing this *being alive* thing for a while now, and I've learned something: If I leave a detail out of a question, it's going to take longer to get a complete answer. While I was writing the description, I anticipated every detail I thought would be relevant.

Ed the Glass Guy replied.

> "For a 9' by 8½' window, it'll be $342.54. Is it on the first floor? Will we need a ladder?"

So many problems.

That's a price for a nine-foot by eight-and-a-half-foot window. That is not a price for the nine-*inch* by eight-and-a-half-*inch* window I asked about. Ed failed to say when he could schedule the service. And he wanted to know if my one-story house has a second-story living room window.

It does not. Thanks for asking.

I could tell a lot of stories about communication issues. I chose this one because it hits all the core points. It shows clear thinking. It shows complete and correct writing. It shows the anticipation of Ed's questions. And it shows complete and utter failure despite all that.

Here's how the elements of communication break down and why they're important.

▶ On Clear Thinking

The result of design is communication.

Yes, there are other results. There's productivity. Delight. Satisfaction. Comfort. Familiarity. Lots more. Not one of them is possible without clarity of communication. These other outcomes are each an effect of what's being communicated.

Communication happens whether you like it or not, whether you *mean* it or not. If you chose a particular shade of powder blue as the background for your app, it's now communicating something to your users. You know that. And you know that being a good designer means choosing what and how you communicate *on purpose*.

You know that.

You have a passion for it, in fact. You light up at the sight of a good, "clean" design because of its stunning ability to communicate to you in a pure way. It's that beautiful thing that happens when someone has taken great care to cut out all the noise and distraction and excess from a design and let it speak directly to you in the most efficient and effective and beautiful means possible. It makes you giddy.

I get it. It happens to me too. Just like you, I absolutely love it when a design is able to remain so pure and so clear that it makes me smile every time I use it. One of the joys of being a designer is the pursuit of creating something that has that effect on other people. Something that communicates *that well*.

And yet, this is where a designer's passion for communication tends to stop. It doesn't extend into other forms of communication. A designer's ability to communicate through visuals and function fails to translate to any other medium.

This is a terrible thing. A designer must communicate in so many other ways on a given day. So many opportunities lost.

Writing and Speaking

I can practically guarantee that you do more writing in a day than you do design work. You do more talking. You do more pitching. *More wondering* aloud with coworkers and peers. More speculating. More defending and convincing. So few of these moments, in my experience, are seized with the same vigor for clean communication that you put into a design. So few of them are planned for their purpose, considered for their effectiveness, evaluated for their results.

I have to be honest. Outside of their favorite design software, most designers *suck* at communicating. (This is not always true, of course—some designers communicate well in a variety of mediums—but it is *certainly* common enough to merit this chapter.)

And remarkably few of them know much it's affecting their ability to lead.

This happens because of the thing at the very core of good communication: clear thinking. We don't spend enough time doing it. It's not an easy thing to do, granted, but that is no excuse for failing to try.

Designers far and wide take great care to keep their desks clean, their files organized. They ogle at photos of office desks on furniture sites staged without cables of any kind. They believe in the eventuality of wireless power so that such a thing of beauty might come true. A clean space is a clean mind.

And then they stand up in front of a room full of people and "um" and "uh" and stagger their way through a design pitch. They fumble through vague answers when questioned. They struggle to form any kind of coherent argument about why they did *this* and how *that* will benefit the user. They write an email full of incomplete thoughts, ellipses, grammar and punctuation errors, half answers. They ask questions that have already been answered.

What a mess.

By all evidence, it's much easier to think clearly when working on a design than it is during a design presentation. A client pitch. A phone call. People are visual, after all, and conversation leaves nothing to stare at and to reevaluate and revise so that the version you show someone is a good version. The spoken word, unless you've practiced it beforehand, is a first draft. It's bound to be messy and disorganized.

This is fine in casual conversation. When you want to convince someone of your idea, however, or defend a design or explain why a decision might be good or bad, first drafts, at the very least, need structure. And you have to be able to devise one on the spot. You don't have to know every word of what's about to pour out, but you absolutely should know where you're headed.

This is the first thing I tried to do in the email to Ed the Glass Guy.

Knowing I had a broken pane of glass, my first and more obvious question was about how much it will cost to fix it. Then there was whether or not I could even find a company that does tiny jobs like this. My first mental draft of that email was something like, "I need a pane of glass replaced. Do you handle jobs like this? What are your rates?"

That wasn't going to work. It was a tiny sliver of what I actually wanted to have happen. Ultimately, I wanted the company to come out and replace the glass. So I thought I should be more specific so they would have all the information on which to base their reply. If they didn't do those kinds of jobs, I could always copy and paste my explanation into the form on some other company's website.

Mental draft 2: "I need to replace a pane of glass that's 9" x 8.5". It's from a living-room window in a historic house. The window frame is made of wood. How much might that cost? When are you available?"

Better. But I kept digging. Because of my work with tech users, I've long since learned something important: People think they communicate more than they actually do. They leave out details. They ask half questions. I didn't want to do that. I wanted to give Ed all the information I had.

I landed on the version I sent. It felt complete. It contained every fact I could come up with that might be relevant to Ed.

Clear thinking leads to clear communication.

I developed my clear thought by thinking through all the implications of the subject before contacting Ed. Recounting all the facts. Forming an opinion on what might be useful information. So I was able to send a series of points in a particular order and walk away feeling like I'd said what needed to be said and found clarity.

This was my attempt at communication *by design*.

The skills you apply to design projects can and should be applied to other communication. Doing this dramatically improves your power to lead.

Here's how you get to it, and how it helps.

Thinking in Frameworks

In reaction to almost anything, you'll first have a bunch of scattered thoughts that threaten to ramble and confuse anyone who would hear them. These are not the thoughts you want to put out into the universe. If they're rambling to you, they'll be insufferable to anyone else.

Sadly, this is how most communications go.

Clear thinking comes from applying structure to those thoughts. You get to coherent communication by applying a sort of template to your otherwise disorganized, stream-of-consciousness-style internal monologue.

The template is like a college essay. The kind with a thesis and supporting statements. It starts by setting a direction. It ends with tying up loose ends. It sounds and feels deliberate. And it's received very differently than the disorganized disasters that normally pour out of people's mouths.

You're not going to land on the most coherent form of your points on the first try. It almost never works that way. But it does work by doing what I did back on that mountain as a teenager: Point to a destination, and improvise your way there. No matter what you need to say, take a moment to size up the result and figure out a path toward it. Once you do that, instead of drowning in rambling ideas, you're writing the first draft of an essay. You can speak with a goal in mind. You can write for a result. You can present with a purpose.

Knowing your destination makes your communications deliberate. This is how you'd like to be known as a designer. To get there, it's also how you should want to be known as a person. If you can be deliberate in all aspects of design work and not just in design itself, you will become known as a reliable, steady, mindful person. And that's just the kind of person other people look to.

Christina Wodtke echoed these ideas when I asked her what she thought were the most valuable skills a designer could have that were also the least represented in the design industry. On her list:

> *Communication—verbal and written communication—is incredibly high and remarkably rare and I'm not sure why. If you want your work to go live, you have to present it, and I'm amazed at how poor presentation skills are— setting people up, telling them what kind of feedback you want, explaining your choices, bringing them on the journey.*

What she's talking about is the idea of pointing your design skills at yourself. Learning to apply your design chops to your own day-to-day communication.

Christina continues:

> *It's just a matter of saying, "You know all that stuff I just did with the interface?"—or whatever you're working on—"Now let me apply it to my own personal interface." Let's try to be clear. Let's give a clear call to action. Let's be user friendly. Many designers aren't as user-friendly as they should be.*

▶ On Writing Well

I mentioned writing. Here's why.

First, you do a lot more writing in a given week than designing. It happens in email, on Facebook, on Twitter, in all kinds of places. Those email threads going around the team and between you and your clients are all about putting together the best strategy and best design possible.

Do they say what you want them to say? Really?

Despite this being an era in which we use the written word to communicate more than any point in human history, people seem to have worse writing skills than ever. How many times have you had to reply to an email to ask for clarification? How many times has someone replied to you to do the same? How many times have you just guessed and hoped for the best?

Writing well has so many upsides, it's unbelievable.

Writing is a thinking exercise. When I emailed Ed the Glass Guy, my first draft was mental. The second was written. The third, I sent. I used writing to think through the details. When you lay your thoughts out in words, it's easier to track all of them at once and see what they form.

This is how writers use writing, in fact. Many, if not most, writers consider writing to be the tool they use to *develop* ideas, not just relay them. They write to find out what they think. Writing forces you to have complete thoughts. It forces you to stay on a subject, to think through it completely. Then it allows you to see your whole idea in front of you so you can revise it. Improve it.

Sounds a little like design, eh?

Writing is designing with words. Designing is writing without them.

By design, I wanted to tell Ed the Glass Guy my story and needs and details in the most coherent, clear fashion possible. I used short sentences. Each one contained just one or two facts. Each one used terminology I thought would make sense for a glass repair person. Besides being sure to know and use good form in the first place, I always make a point to proofread my own writing before sending it. A missing comma makes a big difference in written communication.

Simply getting a handle on the basic tools of writing can significantly affect every project you work on. Sentence structure, grammar, punctuation, organization—all of that helps you be clearer with your colleagues about project details. To be more persuasive. To be more deliberate.

And it's not just for the writing, either. Learning to write well helps you think clearly in the first place. It helps you think more clearly in the long term. All these things help each other. Over time, you become able to readily explain any idea you have, any argument you have. There's no stumbling. Just clarity.

If writing is something you struggle with, consider ways to improve at it. Look at writing classes at a local community college. Check out writing courses online, like those offered by Gotham Writers' Professional Development (www.writingclasses.com/classes/catalogue/professional-development). Find writers you like and study the ways they write, the same way you study great designers. Dig up some books on the subject.

My personal favorites are:

- *The Elements of Style,* by William Strunk Jr. and E. B. White (Longman): Even if you just got out of a college English course—especially if—start here. This is a classic book that gets you cutting down on the flourish and passive voice they so appreciate in academia and truck commercials, and get you writing straight, clean, functional sentences that cut to the chase. But be warned: If you stop with this book alone, you'll regret it.

- *On Writing Well,* by William Zinsser (Harper Perennial): Everyone has a book that changed their lives. This is one of mine. It focuses on the principles, methods, and forms of non-fiction writing, and even breaks down what's specific to various types of nonfiction.

- *How to Write a Sentence: And How to Read One,* by Stanley Fish (Harper Paperbacks): If you hated Strunk and White's *The Elements of Style,* this book offers a nice counter to it, tossing out the standard arguments for sheer minimalism and looking into structures and styles that can make your writing not only functional and purposeful but beautiful.

■ *Several Short Sentences About Writing,* by Verlyn Klinkenborg (Vintage): If you get into writing at all—even if you don't—nothing will blow your mind more than this one. Nothing will make you a more concise and elegant communicator. Every sentence begins on a new line, a fact that illustrates at every step the effect of a sentence standing on its own. Each one is as pure as can be. It not only teaches you how to write with mastery, it leads by example. (If you've read my tiny tome *The Tao of User Experience,* know that I wrote it immediately after reading *Several Short Sentences About Writing.* I haven't been the same since.)

The books in this list, I swear to you, are the writing equivalent of the best design books you've ever read. They will teach you to design with words.

If you happen to be in a hiring position as a designer, do yourself a favor: Interview only the candidates who write well. You'll be thanking yourself for this for a long time to come.

▶ Mapping Your Message to Their Concerns

There's one other thing I was trying to do when I wrote that list of relevant facts to Ed the Glass Guy: speak to his needs instead of my own. The fact that I was contacting him meant I probably needed glass repair. He knew that the second he got the email. He didn't need to know my backstory—the pigeons, the being crotchety. He needed a list of facts to help him devise an accurate quote so he could get through this interaction and on to the next. His day is about scheduling work.

I imagined being Ed. As Ed, I'd want to know all the details of this job. Where the window is. How I'll access it. What supplies I'll need to replace it. The type of window. The type of frame. All kinds of stuff.

I wanted to be thorough. If I'd sent my first version of that email, Ed's reply would have invariably asked each of these questions, one by one. Nine emails later, I'd be annoyed and wondering how long it could possibly take to have a tiny pane of glass replaced. Maybe I should've called.

I imagined the truck he'd drive. Does it have a ladder on it? Does it *always* have a ladder on it, or will he need to know if he should bring it along or not? You know what they say about assumptions.

My email contained answers to every question I could imagine Ed asking.

No, I've never been a glass repair person. When it comes to what one needs to complete a particular job, I can only guess. But I had to do what I could, because otherwise, we'd be going back and forth all day.

Hence the list. I imagined him sitting at his desk processing all this. The house is one story, so I don't need a ladder. It's a historic house with wooden window frames, so I might need some kind of glue or something. It's this big. It's single-pane. Okay, I think I can answer this question. (That's not quite how it worked out, but I'll get to that problem in a minute.)

I knew what I cared about. To get what I wanted, I needed to care about what *Ed* cared about.

My point here is about a lot more than Ed the Glass Guy. It's about product managers. And CEOs. And executives of all kinds who couldn't care less about design unless it has a positive effect on revenue. And rightly so.

Design in a web context became important when it became clear to executives that users couldn't get through a purchasing process without some of that good-time design stuff happening beforehand. It's still true now. Those executives wouldn't be paying your salary if you weren't contributing somehow to the bottom line. So when you talk to them, what do you think is on *their* minds while you're babbling on about sliders and error messages?

Money.

Many of these people have responsibilities to the company that are tied to their financial outcomes. As in, if a design goes out that causes the loss of a ton of money, it's unlikely you'll get fired as a designer. But your product manager? In some situations, that person could be revising his or her résumé by the end of the day.

Hence, if you want to lead a UX effort, one heck of a way to get their attention is to demonstrate how your recommendations lead to the outcomes *they* care about. If you're trying to talk them out of a bad idea, show them how it might affect the dollar signs at the end of this road.

Not only will this get them listening to you, it will get them seeing you as a pragmatic, responsible, valuable member of a team focused on the right things.

I know. It's a drag. You totally didn't get into the design profession to focus on data and financial outcomes. But this is how maturity works. At some point, you realize that the second you start selling cassette tapes of your garage band, your art becomes a product and not merely a way to vent suburban angst.

Design has a purpose. Always. If it doesn't, it's not design. Your purpose as a designer is to achieve some goal that sits way outside of yourself, for people who are not you. You do this by studying people who are not you, designing for them, speaking in their absence, making decisions on their behalf. But you get it *done* by speaking to the people who are paying for the whole deal. And if they're not on board, you're going nowhere.

This is why it's so important in everyday communication to turn your head toward the people you're speaking to and focus on what *they* care about.

And now that you're busy being aware of this fact and practicing it on a daily basis, do yourself a favor:

Tell everyone else.

If you're a freelancer, you'll find this especially true: A lot of times when people in a business start working on a design project with someone outside of that business, they like to tell the designer what they like and what they want and how they want it done. It's so very assertive of them, which you'd think would be better than working with a client who can't tell you at all what they need. It's not. Not really. It's a symptom of something bad.

It's a symptom of your client's belief that you are designing a site for *them*. You're not. You're designing a site or product that will make their business successful. The stakeholders are not the people the product needs to appeal to. They're the people telling you about the constraints and signing the checks and whose businesses depend on you doing your job well. But to do that, your focus needs to be on those other people in the equation. You're not designing for your client; you're designing for your client's business and your client's users.

It is absolutely in your best interest to make that clear from the very start. No part of you should be worried about resisting a client's idea with cause. That's no way to spend your time. Tell your client in the very beginning that your job is to design something that will help them succeed, and that the tactics you take to do so will not always agree with their desires. Tell them you will always explain your reasons for a recommendation. Tell them you will always *have* reasons for your recommendations. (Then, of course, actually do that.)

Speak to the client's concerns. Then remind the client to focus on the user's concerns.

Learning to Predict the Future

An important part of being able to predict the future is learning to anticipate responses. Sadly, the practice regime for doing this well isn't so easy. It involves a little mastery of something called *situational awareness*.

Situational awareness is the art of being able to recognize what's going on around you and what would occur as a result of a changed variable.

Let's say you're driving to a client meeting. On a motorcycle. With no helmet. And no front brake. And it's nighttime. And you're dressed in all black. And the motorcycle's black. Oh, and your headlight is out.

Yeah, you're probably doomed—unless you have a high level of situational awareness. At its best, this means having an uncanny sense of everything around you, how it affects you at this moment, and how it *could* affect you if anything changes (and you just *know* it will change). That car pulling up to the corner up ahead on the right? What if it pulls out? That stoplight— what if it turns yellow before you pass that sign two blocks down? Will you have enough time to stop? If the truck next to you decides to change lanes, will the driver see you? Situational awareness is how good drivers make the decisions that get them home in one piece. A *lack* of situational awareness is cited as the cause of traffic accidents involving human error.

So right there is a pretty good reason to improve at it. But it can have some benefits to your professional life as well.

The key is that part at the end of my description: "a changed variable."

Variables were a big part of passing high school algebra. A changed variable changed the answer to the equation. They're still a big part of your life now. In any situation, one changed variable can change *everything*.

Imagine you're writing a story. Every detail raises a question I now want answered.

You introduce Jack, who is running. *Why is he running?* Because he's scared. *Of what?* Bears. *OK, so he's in the forest. Why is he there?* He was having a picnic. *By himself?* With a girl. *Where's the girl?* She's dead. *Did the bear kill her?* No, a serial killer did. *This is a very different story than I thought it would be.* Yes, I know.

On and on. Your first fact is Jack, running. It's not enough to tell a story. But every new fact leads to another question, and until they're all answered, you won't know the whole story.

Every statement you make creates a question. Good communicators answer those questions. Good communicators know what changes for the recipient with the introduction of each new piece of information.

When I emailed Ed the Glass Guy, every new piece of information was a changed variable for him. When I said I needed to replace a piece of glass, he'd wonder what kind of glass it was. When I said it was for a single-pane window, he'd wonder how big it was. When I answered that, he'd wonder where the window was in the house. My job as a potential customer—yes, I believe that I have a job as a customer—was to relay all the information Ed would need to help me.

In theory, if I answered all the questions that came up as a result of my facts, until the story came to its natural conclusion, Ed would have all he needed. (That's not how it turned out, but more on that soon.)

This is why communication is like situational awareness. Communication is about knowing what might change as a result of every word, and having a plan to deal with it. And it's about learning how to spot what you're leaving out.

Here's the clincher. The same is true in design.

A design is an ecosystem. Disrupt one thing and you disrupt others. A designer's work is to foresee what will be disrupted and how. And to have a plan for dealing with that change if needed. That notion of a "changed variable" is key to virtually everything you do in design and in communication.

If you master only one thing in this book, let it be communication. Because mastering that will make you naturally better at design.

Reading for Comprehension

Most people seem to believe they're only 50 percent responsible for their communication: their own half. Their jobs are to communicate exclusively what they feel is important, and not what's important to the person they're communicating with.

You are responsible for 100 percent of your communication. If someone has a question, it's generally because you haven't provided the information first. If someone fails to understand, it's generally because you failed to create understanding. And if you fail to absorb something that was made perfectly clear, well, then it's because you weren't listening.

And *man*, that's annoying.

Despite everything—despite employing all the techniques I know to communicate as clearly as possible to Ed, there was one piece of the communication equation I could not control: his ability to read for comprehension.

Ed ignored most of what I'd written. He also assumed I didn't know the difference between markings for feet (indicated by a single quote mark) and inches (indicated by a double quote mark). And he skipped the part where I said I lived in a single-story house. He assumed I needed one giant window rather than what I said I needed—a single pane that goes within a frame composed of multiple small panes of glass.

It's a problem I see a lot these days. It's becoming quite a point of frustration. Without turning into the predictable, crotchety old man who would blame social media and the general narcissism of modern culture as a reason why no one listens to anything but themselves, I'll just skip past that part and point out why it's such a problem.

It will lose you respect.

If the people around you on a design project need to repeat answers and continually remind you of things you should already know, they can't rely you on as a design leader. You can't be trusted if you can't process information.

If you have questions after reading an email, read it again for answers. If you're confused during a conversation, restate what you think you've heard so far. Make it a habit after reading sentences to recite them back to yourself—not literally what they say, but what they mean and what information they convey. Build this muscle. It will serve you well.

Enabling Comprehension

After you practice all these things for a while, with any luck you'll notice a couple of interesting benefits. The first is the inverse of reading for comprehension. It's *enabling* comprehension.

You'll notice over time that the most understandable sentences are the short ones. The ones that contain a single subject, a single verb, a single *point*. You'll notice that lengthy sentences are more difficult to track. Often, by the time you get to the end of one, you've forgotten what happened at the beginning. People write this way a lot when they're trying to demonstrate they're good communicators. They use sentences so dense with facts and big words that everyone struggles to read them. Ironic and sad.

Ernest Hemingway, one of the most revered writers in literary history, wrote at a 4th-grade reading level. It can sometimes be difficult to find a two-syllable word in his writings. He did this not because he read at a 4th-grade level, but because simplicity begets understanding. In fact, very few renowned writers write above an 8th-grade reading level. A short sentence containing plain language and straightforward information, free of flourish, always does the job better.

Once you notice this fact as a recipient of information, you can employ it as a conveyor of information. You can learn to be concise yourself. To help others understand everything you say by untying the knots that are normally part of your everyday conversation and making them meaty through clear, short points composed of simple words and phrases.

Clarity and concision are the essence of clean design because they are clean communication. Learning to read and listen for comprehension teaches you to write and speak for comprehension.

▶ Not Just What, but How and When

I recently did some advisory work with a design agency that had a consistent and exhausting problem. One that was also remarkably easy to solve. And it shows why it matters not only how you communicate, but when.

It was a very small agency with just a few people, and its customers were mainly mom-and-pop shops. Small businesses in small towns. Among the design and development people, the agency included a founder, who primarily handled business development; a project manager, who assigned and managed tasks and timelines; and an account manager, who was the main point of contact for clients once the contract was worked out. All of them had periodic contact with the clients. The designers and developers would collaborate on building things, and everyone else would handle dealing with the clients, who invariably had their lists of self-referential opinions and demands about what should or shouldn't be present on their websites. Sometimes, the designers would take exception—in the interest of good design work—and would make design decisions that contradicted client wishes (for good reason).

After these decisions were implemented, something stupid and awful would happen: The client would come back two days later, angry and strong-willed, armed with all sorts of demands and short-sighted arguments, not the least of which was some version of "I want it done this way."

Either the agency's founder, project manager, or account manager would field and hear out these rants and then translate them into tasks for everyone else, essentially resigning to the idea that the agency's job was to do what the client wanted rather than what was good for the client's business. There was no arguing with the client, they seemed to think. Client wants, client gets.

Quite a lot of things are wrong with this situation, but I'll focus on the one relevant to this chapter.

At some point during those two days between the execution of the designer's decisions and the client's subsequent rant, several people had a chance to lead and failed to do so. They had a chance to call the client, explain the thinking behind the design decisions, and then walk the client through how the decisions were manifested in the site's design. But no one did that. Instead, they left the client to see it for themselves, stew about it for two days, get opinionated, get angry, and get on the phone, leaving everyone at the agency on the defense.

Defense may win football games, but design isn't football, and points are the only way you win anything.

Simply calling the client to talk through the design rationale puts the designer in charge of the situation. When clients make demands that are clearly against their business interests, and against the principles of good design, you need to get out in front of it. You need to be able to explain why things won't work, provide alternatives, and explain why the alternatives are the right direction.

Most of the time, this works. Clients are almost always open to a clear and coherent argument when you can bring one. Even when they're not, this approach puts you in the position of presenting your argument to a calm client rather than an angry one.

It's not just what you say, but when you say it. Saying it two days earlier would have been a simple solution to this agency's recurring anger management problem.

An even better solution would have been to present design decisions like newbie computer users learn to hit Save: early and often.

When you communicate design rationale early and often, the client never gets a chance to disagree with you. They are collaborators rather than enemies. The chance to create this relationship starts at the beginning, during the first conversation. When you communicate the process you've chosen for the project, you give them a path to follow. When you communicate your strategy, you give them a goal to strive for. When you communicate your design decisions at the time you make them, you give them something to agree with.

If this agency started outlining their process at the beginning, and explained decisions before the client saw them, their clients would stop being angry and start being thankful.

When matters just as much as *what*.

Do What You Can

Communication is always incomplete. Short of climbing inside a person's brain, you'll never get all of what they mean to say, nor will you ever be able to fully predict all of what you need to say to be 100 percent understood. But holding yourself accountable for as much of it as you can will certainly change the nature of your conversations. If you walk into every interaction with the idea that it is your job to be complete, your job to understand the recipient's needs as well as your own, and your job to receive information as well as you deliver it, you will put yourself in a position to lead.

Don't take this lightly. You're in the communication business. To be good at anything, you'll need to be good at this.

If you can think clearly, you can communicate clearly. And if you can communicate clearly, you can lead. Because communicating well buys you something you can't get in any other design deliverable:

Trust.

7

Arguing

- ▶ Listening
- ▶ Asking
- ▶ Educating
- ▶ Presenting
- ▶ Backing It Up

In 2005, I was running a UX team and in need of another designer or two. I wrote up a job description, handed it off to HR to post to the company website, and waited for the fantastic candidates to come running, résumés in hand. The first one I got was from a guy on one of the product development teams—a programmer who had recently become enthralled by design and wanted a chance to dig in. Seemed he'd been hovering around the Jobs section of the company site waiting for just such an occasion. As soon as it showed up, he clicked the button.

I'm the type who hires from all directions. The way I see it, a person can get better at the more readily learnable aspects of UX as long as that person has the intense curiosity and other qualities so crucial for a good designer. That same year, for example, I hired someone with fairly poor design chops, but who was hooked on it like a drug and who had a Cognitive Psychology degree—a combination that's pretty hard to find. I'm not afraid, in other words, to teach someone who has the built-in gusto and smarts. A designer can always get better. They can't always grow more brain cells or become more naturally ambitious.

Besides that, I was a programmer once (a three-year case of *designer, interrupted*). I could identify with a guy who wanted to break out and challenge himself.

So I scheduled the interview.

He got through some of the questions well enough, albeit a bit nervously. He clearly had no design experience, but he'd been reading books and had become somewhat awestruck by the complexities of form design and the notion of making everything simpler. He was at that point where we all start—the one where he would see bad things and point them out to other people and complain about them. When you don't know what happens next, that's what you do—complain. It was fine. I could work with that as long as he cared.

After a while, I said to him that a lot of design was about being able to demonstrate that your recommendations are worth considering, and I asked how he approached convincing people of the merits of his ideas. He was a programmer, after all—surely he'd had to do this before.

Part of his response was a sentence that's stuck in my memory ever since:

"Well, I'm usually pretty good at waving my arms around and screaming until I get people listen to me."

He waved his arms around while saying it as if to prove he could. And indeed, he seemed capable of some perfectly suitable arm-waving.

I didn't hire him, though. The arm-waving just wasn't as compelling as I wanted it to be. It wasn't the fluidity or style so much. It was the sheer lack of rhetoric in his response that his arm-waving was trying to keep me from noticing. If his rhetoric was a total non-starter in an interview—where he was supposed to be presenting an argument for why I should hire him—it's unlikely he'd be able to help me convince the massive engineering team at this company that design mattered.

Why has this story been stuck in my head for so long?

Because for all the ridiculousness of this story, I haven't met many designers who could've answered the question any better.

Rhetoric

You know that nervous feeling you get when you call a client to recommend something? It's because you know they're going to wonder why, and you're going to have to spit out some sort of explanation. And that explanation is going to be rooted mostly in rationale such as "that's how it's usually done" and "I think this is the way to go." And you're going to stutter through it. You're going to dance around the answer in some weird circle of words that starts and ends with the same vague stumbling sounds.

A lot of times, your client will buy it, but they'll wonder why they're playing along. They'll suspend disbelief for a while. And then, at the end of the process, they'll decide whether they're happy with your work. Your guess is as good as mine as to whether or not they will be.

Such a terrible feeling. Such a terrible situation to know you're going to face even once, let alone on every project. So why do you keep doing it?

There's a better way.

Instead of floundering, you could make that phone call with a solid argument in your back pocket. Just as with the template I talked about in the previous chapter for turning incoherent thoughts into an ordered, logical narrative, you can devise an effective pitch for your recommendations by thinking through the *why* behind each one and organizing it into a case.

Start by disallowing yourself use of any variation of the words "That's the way it's always been done" or "That's how other people do it" or "It's best practice." These words are crutches. It's bad enough to rely on these non-arguments in your design work. It's far worse to make your clients endure them and simply trust you know what you're doing.

To truly convince a client, nothing beats a lucid, coherent argument based on evidence and which considers the project's surrounding factors.

Rhetoric is one of the most important skills you can have as a designer. Besides being in the communication business, designers are in the persuasion business. How can a design do its job if it can't convince people to use it? How can designers be effective if they can't convince people of their insights and ideas?

And yet.

Even those who are capable of being persuasive don't necessarily know how they're doing it. Or how vital persuasive skills are to their jobs. Or why.

Mastering rhetoric is essential to leading. It means you can finally come back with a good argument rather than succumbing to what they tell you to do. It gives you the power and confidence to take a stand, and to even make a recommendation in the first place. Knowing things isn't enough. You have to be able to communicate them. No matter what you do, you're in Sales.

This chapter is on some of the techniques for being able to make the sale.

▶ Listening

Once, an agency I was working with handed me the most straightforward brochure-ware site project that could exist. The client was an independent B2C reseller of home construction materials. Simply, they bought the products from manufacturers and wholesalers and resold them directly to consumers through a large warehouse. It was a basic retail business.

When the agency asked me to help out, I was told that all the client needed was a basic design for a few pages about the company and what they did—that's all. The client generally helped its customers in person, not online, so the site was more just for sharing high-level information, not specifics. UX-wise, it was barely a project. This would be a simple matter of figuring out what message and information the client wanted to get across, and then designing a few pages around that. It would take a day at most.

When I called the client to talk through it, I started out by asking a few questions about the business and its workings, and the client's goals for the website. That's when the person on the other end of the call said something a little incongruent with the agency's assessment of the situation:

"We want to use the site to replace the brochures we use now when we're walking around the yard with customers."

I asked more questions. Like, "I'm sorry, what?"

By the end of the call, the project had completely changed shape. This client wanted to shift from a paper brochure-based process of walking around and talking to customers and writing notes and filling out forms to one where the sales staff used iPads to select the precise products the customer wanted and built an estimate for those products with the option to order them right then and there.

Oh. Well then. That would take a bit more work. I wondered if the agency knew exactly what the client wanted.

"Did you know the client wants to put its entire brochure online and enable its salespeople to use iPads to put together estimates and submit orders?" I asked.

"Um, no," the agency said. "That would be a much bigger project than what they told us before."

It wasn't a much bigger project than what the client had told the agency before. It was a much clearer *understanding* of what the client wanted than what the agency had *heard* before.

See the difference? It's another testament to the value of listening. Oftentimes, your client is trying to tell you things they don't know how to express. Your job as a designer is often to pick through the subtleties and pull out the truths they're not being explicit about.

The client had said all this previously. Perhaps not in the same words, because people get better at explaining things over time and are not always so good on the first try. But they'd said it perhaps with exactly the same amount of stress. Which is to say: very little.

The client hadn't started out the call this way. I'm not sure he even knew he needed to stress what he wanted. It's quite likely he knew exactly what he wanted, but no idea that the *agency* didn't know. The agency, apparently, was supposed to have read the client's mind or something. Clients often believe that.

"He'd said something like that before," the agency told me, "but I guess I thought that was a long time off. It didn't really make sense with what he was saying."

Clearly there was a communication gap. Perhaps they should've read Chapter 6 first.

Regardless of what happened, it reminded me of an important aspect of design: Before you can make a case for any kind of solution, you need to know what the problem is. And that means *listening.*

Yeah, yeah. Everyone's always telling you to listen. Listen to your clients. Listen to your users. Listen to your significant other. They've been talking about listening since you were in kindergarten. Everyone wants to be heard, no one wants to listen.

I don't want to pile on here, but they've got a point. When it comes to forming a good argument, listening is pure gold. I walked into that call believing I understood the situation and just needed some additional information to get started. By the end, I was working on a *very* different project. One that would be worth a lot more money.

It pays to listen.

(That won't be literally true if you're an in-house designer with a set salary, but you get the idea.)

Listening helps you determine what the constraints of a project really are. What the client's concerns and goals really are. It helps you see whether or not you've already got the right argument in hand or if it needs revising before you can know exactly what to argue for.

It also helps put the client into a different mindset. Restating what you've heard back to the person you're listening to is arguably the #1 way to make a client feel receptive to the ideas you're about to present. It shows respect. It shows that your forthcoming recommendations will be tightly relevant to the client's needs.

▶ Asking

Once, during an event in Austin, Texas, I was sitting on a stool at the front of a room next to Harry Max, then the VP of Design for Rackspace. He's the man who will be forever known for designing the web's first shopping cart. We'd given our talks, and the floor was open for questions. A few dozen sets of eyes were staring at us, and neither of us had any idea what question would come next. The third or fourth one was a nerve-shaker.

"How do you know who to hire?"

As in, when you bring in a gaggle of UX candidates to meet people, shake hands, and answer questions, how do you know which one is good and which one is terrible when you don't know the first thing about UX or how to evaluate its success?

It was one of the best questions I've ever been asked by an audience member.

It's not an easy one to answer. Volumes could be (and have been) written on what UX really means, and why, and how far it reaches into the business and what skills you actually need for *your* business or for *this* project. And the people who claim UX in their title, as I've discussed, have a huge range of backgrounds. Some have a degree in cognitive psychology and are experts in usability. Some just walked out of graphic design school yesterday. Even someone who's been doing it for years may have just come from an organization that thinks the UX person is nothing more than a glorified wireframer. Hiring managers need to be able to discern one from the other.

You can go by the candidate's job history, sure. But it won't tell you how good that person has gotten through those experiences. Some people can do a lot with very little experience. Some get almost nowhere with a ton of experience.

Portfolios are better than job histories. But only if the candidate can talk through what they did in each portfolio example. Designers need to be able to talk through how they approached the problem and then map the project's goals to the design, and the design decisions to the project's outcomes. Otherwise, the portfolio is useless. You can't tell what a UX professional did on a project by looking at screenshots. The designer has to tell the story.

Even when the designer can tell a good story and walk through the whole process with grace and clarity, one thing stands above both portfolios and job histories.

It's the one and only way to pick a great UX professional—or one with the potential to be great—out of a lineup.

Look for the person asking all the best questions.

Don't stress one part of that sentence over another. There are two key parts to this idea: *all* and *best*.

As I discussed in Chapter 5, a UX person asks questions—about the users, the business, the concerns, the needs, the prior decisions, the team, the goals. A great UX person wants to see the whole picture. They ask questions because they're intensely curious. They ask questions because the answers can help them see what they're getting into. They ask questions because they want to work toward a vision for the project they can use to make good design decisions.

Simply asking questions lets them do all that. And one more thing.

Asking questions lets a designer *form a coherent argument*. Asking is as important as listening. It's *part* of listening. Asking means dragging more and more information out into the sunlight where it can have holes poked in it and arguments formed for and against it.

The designer who asks is the designer who learns.

Next time you walk into an interview, ask a ton of questions. Next time you need to make an informed decision (which is, like, every day as a designer), ask a ton of questions. Next time you need to fend off a bad idea, a whim, someone's bias, your *own* bias, ask a ton of questions.

Phases of Knowledge

In conversations I've had with Harry Max since that night, we've talked some about communication. He's the one who first articulated to me the idea that people are 100 percent responsible for their communication, whereas they think they are only 50 percent responsible. He's also the one who articulated something I'd never thought about—the *process* of questioning.

People go through phases of knowledge, he explained. At first, you're in a state of Unconscious Incompetence. Basically, you don't know what you don't know. A hefty number of facts exist about a subject, and you don't know what they are or that they even exist. During this time, you ask a lot of general questions. These questions are like a musket; they shoot pellets in all directions with the hope of hitting a big, broad area.

Unconscious Incompetence → Conscious Incompetence → Conscious Competence → Mastery

The more these questions get answered, the more you move toward Conscious Incompetence. At this stage, you get an idea of how much you don't know. You start to see the size and scope of the subject, and realize just what you have a grasp on and what you don't. Your questions start to focus on specific aspects of the subject so you can learn more about each one as you think it's relevant.

Gradually, you move into Conscious Competence. This means you have a decent knowledge of the subject field and can actually perform within it. You can speak with some intelligence about the subject, consider the details in more depth, take action, make decisions.

This can happen in a single conversation. For a small subject, you can find your way into a working knowledge pretty quickly. For a big topic, it can take weeks. Months. Years.

For a career, this usually takes years. When you start design school, you're at the stage of Unconscious Incompetence. By the time you graduate, you should be nearing a state of Conscious Incompetence. You know things now, but you probably won't be able to understand or do them really well for a while. A year or two in, depending on how well you learn and what kinds of projects you've gotten in on, you can approach Conscious Competence.

What *can't* happen in a single conversation, or even months, is Mastery, the final phase. This comes after years of asking questions and working and building experience and examining all sides of your subject. According to the oft-cited book by Malcolm Gladwell—*Blink*—it takes upwards of 10,000 hours to achieve Mastery. For most people, that's *years'* worth of work.

No matter what you're applying this model to, it centers on questions. Every bit of learning you do in your life involves asking and answering questions, even if they weren't explicit, even if you didn't set out to learn anything. You could be reading the news one day with no particular desire and end up learning the answer to a question you didn't even know you were asking.

Answers give you fuel. They form your opinions. They provide evidence you can cite. They let you form an argument.

In practical terms, consider how this works at the beginning of a project:

At first, you ask a lot of broad questions. The more you learn, the more specific your questions get. The more you ask, the more armed you become with information that qualifies you to make decisions.

A good UX pro always wants to get to Conscious Competence. A great one wants to get to Mastery.

Restating

Some quick advice to take full advantage of the answers you get:

Restate them. As in, out loud. For several reasons.

First, it helps the person answering your question know you've heard them correctly. Second, it ensures *you* understand the answer. Third—and this isn't incredibly common, but it certainly happens from time to time—restating the answer you hear can cause the person who provided the answer to rethink it. Simply hearing it said back forces the person to recognize some flaw in the logic they couldn't hear when the answer was still hidden away inside their own brain.

▶ Educating

Unbelievably, I recently had a client ask me to add "click here" to a proposed link. She was worried the user wouldn't know I meant for them to click—the link was a question like "Forgot password?" I explained the reasons for not including "Click here."

First, I explained how the convention began. In the early days, millions of people were using the Internet for the first time every day, and a lot of web designers thought it was somehow their job to teach people how to use their particular website through explicit design elements like "click here," as if the user hadn't already had to *click here* a thousand times just to get to the website in the first place. We said things like, "Need help? Click here to contact us." It turns out, we could have just said, "Contact us."

Then I explained screen readers. I pointed out that quite a lot of people have some kind of visual impairment that results in them needing to use a screen reader, and that when you're using a screen reader, "click here" means nothing. It does nothing to help the user know what the link goes to. Hence, using "click here" could mean decreasing usability rather than increasing it.

Finally, I explained a more subjective point: "click here" is an old convention, and if we were to use it now, the site could look outdated.

Yes, it takes time to explain things like this. That email took 20 minutes to write.

But it's always worth it. It buys you respect, and it shows your client respect. What they hear is that you care enough to explain your rationale. It also demonstrates that you *have* a rationale—a deep, considered rationale—for everything you do. It builds trust.

Some days, your best arguments don't mean a thing. Your clients, coworkers, and other stakeholders want to do what they want to do no matter how potent your case is for doing it another way. Your research goes to waste. Your evidence goes limp in the face of whim and obstinacy.

This is usually a timing problem (see the "Not Just What, but How and When" section in Chapter 6). Generally, though, taking the time to explain your rationale will settle any nerves a stakeholder might have.

In all, educating your clients and coworkers and stakeholders with every recommendation you make has several major effects:

- It guarantees you have a reason for your recommendation. If you can explain it, you've thought it through.

- It gives everyone else a good reason for the recommendation. (Often, they just need to know there is a reason.)

- It has a great long-term effect: It teaches people to think about design. To think like a designer. To think like a user. It teaches them that every decision has an impact on a user's experience and therefore should be considered. Do this well, and over time you won't need to form an argument for your recommendations nearly as often. The people around you will have learned to make better design decisions in the first place.

The benefits of education are far more valuable than the time it takes to do the educating.

▶ Presenting

Building on the story about the design agency in the previous chapter—
the one that let its clients review unexplained work and decide they hated
it—let's look at some effective *methods* for explaining your work. In your
career, you'll get plenty of chances to do exactly that—like, on every project. You might be in a conference room full of stakeholders who need to
hear your proposed solutions. You might be on stage at a web conference.
You might be in a meeting with a lone design manager who just wants to
see how a project is developing. You may just need a second opinion. No
matter the situation, it helps to follow a path.

If you can present your case well and do it up front, you don't need to argue.
Your narrative will address every concern before it even comes up.

It looks something like this.

First, remember what I said in Chapter 6: It helps to apply an essay-like
structure to your communication. When you're presenting design work to
someone, that college essay structure can be pure gold. Besides giving you
a template to follow, it's a template that works well. It's time-tested. Its
structure of thesis–support–conclusion tells a story to the recipient.

Speaking of stories.

Explaining with Stories

Stories are fantastic for grounding your recommendations in reality as you
explain them. To demonstrate this, I'll make the rest of my points here
through a story that illustrates a time I've followed my own advice.

A couple of years ago, I worked on one of those rare projects that actually
had the budget and time for user research. Minimal user research, but user
research nonetheless.

At the beginning of the project, during the strategy-definition phase,
I started out with the usual discovery process: stakeholder interviews,
debriefing on all the past decisions, determining the scope of the existing

app and the hopes for its future, things like that. I gathered a list of a few recommended and trusted power users who were generally receptive to giving their feedback to the product team. Since they were all remote, I scheduled Skype calls with them. Before I spoke to them, I was told that although these few users were generally helpful, they also "hate change."

You know that phrase. It's the one every design team seems to believe but is never actually true. People don't hate change. They hate badly executed change. Generally, the problem isn't the users. It's the design teams who don't know how to introduce change and demonstrate its value.

I spoke to them all on the same day. In the interest of being respectful of their time, I came prepared. I kicked off each call with a summary of why I was calling, what I was hoping to learn, and a series of questions. I had very few questions, but an hour to spend with each person. I did this so that there was time for improvisation. Walk in with too many questions and you leave no time for conversation. The best insights I've ever gained from users have invariably come in the comments on things I didn't ask about. They say something curious, I ask more about it, and it turns out the team is missing something vital (like the client I described before who actually wanted a massive online catalog but didn't know how to express that fact).

These conversations went well. I asked my questions, they gave their answers, and I ended up with a ton of insight and information I didn't know existed and hadn't set out to get. I ended each call with a solid feeling that I understood what they really felt was missing from the app, the ways it was failing them, and so on. (And of course, their recommendations on how to fix those problems, generally, were things that would just cause *other* problems.)

A week or so later, I had a solid strategy document and I started working on some low-fi wireframes. Nothing vivid, just some basic ideas. With each one, I considered what was at the root of the problems and hopes described by the users I'd spoken to, the product team, and the company's more executive stakeholders. Multiple times, I found that the design couldn't simply be tweaked and rolled out slowly. Parts of it would have to be entirely redesigned. This meant I'd have to go back to these people who "hate change" and get them onboard.

There is no magic trick to this. No sleight of hand. Rolling out significant change is a strategic exercise.

I got back on Skype with each one of them. During each call, I recapped what the person had told me previously: the problems they'd identified, the concerns they had, the changes they'd suggested. Each person had a few. As I did, they each nodded their heads up and down. *Ah, yes,* they seemed to say. *Those are all, in fact, problems I've seen.* Once I had the person nodding, I went through the design and showed—in the same order—how the new design approached those issues.

To prove to myself and to them that the new design was better, I didn't *just* explain my solutions. I ran a micro usability test. I showed a screen to the person and asked how he or she would perform a particular task. Each time, they answered without pause. The new design was indeed working just great. Then I explained how the new design was different and how the design either dealt with or entirely eliminated the problems they had expressed. This resulted in a lot more nodding.

By the end of each call, I had validated several design ideas, run a preliminary usability test, and earned buy-in from someone who had purportedly *hated change.* Since these were power users who had the attention and respect of a *ton* of other users, this plan also meant we'd be able to roll out changes one at a time and count on these power users to be advocates for them.

Get the right few people on your side in the beginning and you get everyone else on your side later on.

To sum up: I used the research to inform the strategy, I used the strategy to make the design decisions, and I used the design decisions to show the power users how their problems would be solved.

This is how a UX project is supposed to go.

There was just one more thing I needed to do before we could all plow forward on design and development: I had to convince the team of my conclusions and recommendations. So next came the slide deck.

I spent an afternoon putting together an Apple Keynote deck reviewing the strategy, describing the calls I'd had with each user, and then walking through how the wireframes addressed these issues and supported the long-term goals for the product. More nodding.

Along the way, besides describing the connections between my design decisions and the strategy document, I told stories. I talked about what the users I'd interviewed had said, how they'd grunted or laughed over certain topics, the words they'd used to express their frustrations. I gave my impressions of each person. Basically, I made those four power users part of every topic.

Developers asked questions. Designers asked questions. The data analyst asked questions. I dealt with each one either with evidence, a story about a user, or something else.

It would be months before the more significant design changes had been built out and deployed, but by the end of that hour, the nerves seem to have been calmed.

The next day, I heard from the product manager that several members of the team had stopped by her office to express their sheer excitement over the coming months. They said it was the best experience they'd had with a UX professional. The morning after that, the product manager asked if I'd consider joining the team full time. (I had to decline. I'm not a one-company kind of guy.)

This is clearly a very different experience than the ones being had by the little agency with the angry clients. But it had nothing to do with me. I cannot make people who "hate change" magically believe in the joy of disruption.

It's all in the communication strategy, which was derived from a long line of people and situations over the years I've been in this profession. I learned from one person that change rolled out slowly, one piece at a time, can be much more acceptable to users than massive change all at once. I learned from project work that turning a few users into advocates can make a world of difference when it comes to user acceptance on flip-the-switch day. I learned that mapping your decisions to users' frustrations is one heck of a way to get them nodding their heads.

Add them all together and you get a strategy for rhetoric that involves no arguing whatsoever.

You listen. You ask questions. You make decisions based on evidence. You explain the evidence for every decision. You present your case by describing the strategy, mapping every decision to it, and telling stories about how you arrived at your conclusions. And you get advocates on your side.

This chapter may be about how to argue well, but when you do all this, you don't need to argue at all.

Leading the Room

Here's one crucial tip for how to keep an audience captive while you're making your case. A lot of times, your audience, especially the smaller ones of just a few people, will want to ask questions along the way. This can be fine if it's a minor question with a quick answer. But if they nail you with something you need to think about or that a bunch of other people have an opinion on, you can find yourself in the weeds in no time. There is no quicker way to derail your coherent argument than to let something like this distract you and leave everyone forgetting what you were hoping to achieve.

The tip is pretty simple:

Ask people to hold their questions until the end. Tell them to write their questions down and that you'll get to them. Tell them you've planned for that. Then stick to your promise; leave plenty of time for them to ask.

In many cases, especially if you've done your job well of predicting the future, you'll end up answering most of the obvious questions along the way. This doesn't mean you're done, however. It's practically a guarantee that someone will ask you something you haven't yet considered. This is what Q&A is for.

If you let these things throw you off your track in the middle of the meeting, you may never answer all the other important questions. If your meeting is an hour, leave 10 minutes at the end for questions. If you're running more of a feedback or review session, leave more time.

Whatever the case, *leave time*. Questions are the only way you'll know what you've missed.

▶ Backing It Up

There is one other way to argue without arguing.

I've advocated the use of evidence time and time again in this book. I'm going to do it once more.

Evidence can come from a lot of places. It can be a study you read about on a psychology website. It can be personal observation (which becomes more credible the more experienced you get as a designer). It can be the results of a usability test. It can be data you recalled from a previous project that involved a similar design problem. It doesn't really matter where it came from as long as it's credible, its conclusions are relevant, and you can connect the dots between the evidence and your current project.

Evidence has, of course, several major benefits. For starters, it means you can make a case to *yourself.*

It can become really easy over time to accept your previously learned lessons as standing truths. Not only that, but *universal* truths. You think that thing you learned five years ago is not only still true, it's true in every situation. Let's say, for example, you once witnessed five people in a row ignore a line of instructions on a form. It's easy to believe it will keep happening. But as you work through more and more projects, you'll need to test this notion many times. A line of instructive text isn't just a line of instructive text. It's a font. It's a color. It's something a user can skip past, stuffed between two fields in light gray and a 6pt font.

It's a visual element as much as it is text. A user's bypassing of it is no sign of universal truth. Moved to a different spot, given a different color, its font size bumped up a notch or two, it could be just what the user needs. Displayed inside a big purple box right next to the form as the user clicks the field it relates to, it could be impossible to ignore. In a different *application*—one where the information the form asks for is complicated and needs to be looked up—it could be consistently sought out. Every standard has exceptions. Designers tend to think users avoid reading while they're performing tasks. But it's certainly not always true. And if you're working on such a project, ignoring this fact could be a major detriment. Gathering some data on your assumptions early on can mean big differences in your design's effectiveness.

No matter how much you believe something, data can prove you wrong. Every suspicion, every assumption, every guess can be validated or debunked with a little research. And the last thing you want is to recommend a false truth. When you feel like you know you're right, take some time to make sure. See if the studies covered in articles online still back you up. See if the data you have access to can verify your belief.

I can't tell you how many times—especially early on in my career—I learned something only to unlearn it later. The older I've gotten, the more I've recognized that there are no hard and fast answers. Every decision you make is a guess. Your job is to mitigate the risk of that guess as much as you can. If you're unsure about something—if you *are* sure about something—find evidence to prove it, one way or another. This will give you a great deal of confidence about your recommendations. All you have to do to convince someone after that is relay the facts.

Hence, my second point:

Data helps you make the case for your recommendation to everyone else, especially after you've vetted it yourself. Remember: This book is about how to lead as a UX professional. If you're out front with all the facts in your hand, and you've considered your recommendations, and you can demonstrate their validity, people will believe you. They'll believe *in* you.

Finally, putting evidence up for examination with every recommendation you make will build your reputation over time. It'll become easier and easier to get past whatever obstacles you face now. The objections. The politics. People will learn they have a trustworthy source of reliable, accurate information in their midst, and they'll come to rely on it rather than their guesses.

This will take a long time. But if you stick to it, it will work.

Always point to evidence. Always *have* evidence to point to.

This chapter has been about ways to fit rhetoric into your projects, but it's most certainly terrible as a course on rhetoric itself. For a look at the actual techniques and elements of rhetoric, I highly recommend the book *Thank You for Arguing*, by Jay Heinrich (Three Rivers Press, 2007). It's a quick read, it introduces all the basics, and in it, the author uses references to conversations with his kids a few times as real-life examples of rhetoric, which makes the whole thing personable too.

8

Leading

▶ Staying Calm

▶ Ignoring Distractions

▶ Speaking Up

▶ Taking Criticism

▶ Being Collaborative

▶ Hiring Well

▶ Offering Solutions Instead of Complaints

▶ Giving Credit Away

▶ Teaching Them to Teach

▶ Managing Things Away from People

▶ Creating Opportunities for Others

▶ Choosing Teams Over Individuals

In the years I've been in the web industry, I've held exactly two in-house leadership positions as a UX director. Prior to the first, I worked in a variety of roles, including graphic designer, programmer, courseware designer, and a lot more, eventually working my way into the Director chair at a good-sized, market-dominating software company. I stayed for one year. Nine or so years later, I joined a startup for a few months as UX director, but then left after deciding I didn't want to relocate. During the nine years between, and in the time since, I've been a UX strategy consultant. This has involved working with dozens—possibly many dozens—of companies, temporarily running design projects and design teams, sometimes for a few days, frequently for a few weeks, and once in a while for several months.

I've had a lot of practice, in other words, walking into situations and drowning in them for a minute until I was able to find my footing and start getting things done.

It's not always hard to do, but it's also not always easy. The pressure is usually on from the first day to forge a path, lead the way, and get everyone else to follow. Usually, I have a tiny amount of time during which to make a solid impression, build rapport, and earn trust. If I don't, projects can go wrong. If I do, I have the chance to leave lasting guidelines in place that will shape a product or team for months or years to come.

So I've had to learn to do this well. I've had to learn to do this fast. I've had to learn to do it consistently, no matter how different the situation might be from the last or all the others before it.

In each and every situation, the qualities and actions I've discussed throughout this book have been crucial to success. Being able to cite evidence when making recommendations. Listening. Researching. Having a general knowledge of many subjects and deep knowledge of a few. Being able to adapt and work within any set of constraints. Understanding psychology. Learning to present well.

All these things factor in to whether or not I'll be able to make something great happen in the time I have with a client. And while all of them contribute to being a leader and help you build credibility and trust, a few skills, I think, are specific to leaders.

I've seen these skills from all sides. I've had bosses, I've been the boss, and I've worked with other people's bosses. (A *lot* of other people's bosses.) Product managers. Project managers. UX team leads. Directors. VPs. CTOs. CEOs. They've had a lot of titles. They've all been managers of some kind.

Very few of them have been *leaders*.

And strangely, very few of the leaders have been bosses.

I know. It's all so counterintuitive. But I'm betting you've spotted these qualities in people who weren't bosses a few times yourself. I'm betting you've really liked working with them. I'm betting you've wished the people who are your bosses were more like them.

If you were lucky enough to work with one, I'm betting you stayed. If you left, I'm betting it's because you learned so much from this person that you felt it was time to hold yourself to the standard that person held you to.

I can name the leaders I've had as bosses on one hand. I can't even count, though, the times I've seen glimpses of these great qualities in other people.

My point?

You are in a position to lead. It doesn't matter what your title is. It doesn't matter if you're someone's boss. Or have some incarnation of a manager's job title. What matters is that you want good UX to happen. You want to raise the bar. You want to push your potential forward, and everyone else's along with it.

You can do that.

Here's how.

▶ Staying Calm

In my early 20s, I worked as the assistant manager of a video store with one of the best managers I've ever had. Her name was Kim. She was in her late 30s at the time, wore the video store costume every day just like the rest of us, and carried around a large ring of keys on her belt. It was out of sheer necessity. Video stores require a lot of keys.

When she dished out instructions to team members, as was a big part of her job, she had this way of standing. She'd stand slightly turned, one foot ahead of the other, with her forward shoulder tilted down and her head down. Then she'd look directly at you and say something like, "When you get a chance, can you please clear that shelf and put out the new releases?"

At the time, I struggled to explain what it was about this stance of hers that was so powerful. It never felt condescending or cold. It never felt angry or harsh. It didn't even feel commanding. It felt like she was telling you a secret. Like she wanted you to carry out that task because you were the only one who could. You were the go-to guy. She trusted you.

After a long time, I realized it wasn't the stance so much. It was her entire demeanor. When she asked people to complete tasks, when she asked how your life was going, when she mentioned something her family had done last week, when she asked how the event was that you went to last night, she did it with the same steady, calm tone she used in every other situation. The woman's heart rate never went up. She was as even-keeled as it gets. Deliveries would arrive. Customers would ask questions. Lines would get long. Her voice never rose. Kim simply did not believe in anxiety.

And everyone loved her.

Not one person on that staff ever had a bad thing to say about Kim. They happily carried out every task. They took on more responsibility when it was needed without question, eager to do it. They spoke highly of her. They showed up on time. They headed home for the night without stress.

We threw a party for her when she left to go another company. A celebration over a boss is not the kind of thing that happens a lot in retail work.

What I'm about to say is potentially some pretty basic pop psychology, but it needs to be pointed out. Not a lot of people, in my experience, are so great at stepping outside of themselves and looking back in to evaluate their own behavior or its effects. Here goes:

We teach other people how to treat us.

When we jump out of our seats at the slightest jostling, we teach people to yell "Boo!" When we get and stay anxious, we teach people to avoid us. When we push things off, we teach people they can't trust us. When the CEO postpones everyone's favorite project for three weeks to deal with legacy issues on a product you're phasing out anyway and you sigh and roll your eyes, you teach the CEO to treat you like a nuisance rather than a leader.

When we are calm, and steady, and even, and *consistent* (as in, there are few or no exceptions to this behavior), we teach people we can be relied on. That we are capable of handling any challenge. That we can be trusted as leaders.

The way you act and react affects the way everyone else will see you the next time they need you to act or react. Stay calm in all situations, and you will have all the respect you'll ever need to get things done when the chance comes.

▶ Ignoring Distractions

This one I learned while working at a startup as UX director.

As a startup, we had one product, but we were nearing a point where it would split into two. The company would eventually focus all its energy on the second, realizing it had far more potential than the first. When I joined the company, it was with the intent to invent and shape that second product while also getting the first product into good enough condition that it could just sit there, functioning and making money—for a good long time—and generating revenue to support the second product's ramp-up period. The original product wouldn't take much attention, we thought—it had already been up and running for a couple of years and was fairly stable. But I'd be lying if I said it didn't take more than its share of our resources. For every day we should have been working on the second product—the new one that would be company's future—we ended up spending much more than that dealing with the problems of the first product. Technical debt. Bugs. Features we had to add to make it competitive. It may have been around for a couple of years, but it turned out to be in worse shape than anyone realized.

So for the second time in my career, rather than work on an array of projects, I had an in-house position with a single mission. The first time had been to start and run the UX team and work it into an engineering-centric process. This time it was to invent a product without letting its predecessor drive me out of my skull.

Practically every single day, something would come up to keep me from making as much progress as I would've liked. So-and-so, our biggest customer, would have three new demands for what the flagship product should do. The lead architect would tell us about some newly discovered piece of the system in desperate need of overhauling and that it would prevent the dev team from working on the new product. The CEO would announce he was heading to a conference and would need a prototype in hand to show off some future revision we hadn't planned to complete until sometime much later. Then someone on the core strategy team (besides me, this included the product manager, the CEO, and the CTO) would second-guess a previous decision, and I'd have to spend an hour selling them on it all over again.

It never ends in startups.

Distraction after distraction after distraction.

The amazing thing is, not one of them bothered me. Sure, some days were more frustrating than others. But even on the worst day, I still had one goal. I was there to turn that second product into a reality. Every other thing that happened was a distraction.

It would be a long road. It would require resources we didn't yet have. It would take a lot of convincing and testing and validating and research and design. But it would happen. It was my job to make it happen. And tunnel vision can have a remarkable effect on a person.

Not every situation has a singular purpose. I fully concede that. When you're in an agency situation, or are the sole designer for several products at once, it can be trying on the best days to stay focused. But even within those roles, one project is often bigger, more important, a bigger accomplishment than the others. If it's not a project, maybe it's a career goal. A strategic shift. A cultural shift. There's always something to focus on that means more than all the rest of it.

Put your energy there. It's what lets you ignore the distractions. And ignoring distractions is what lets you stay calm.

There are a million distractions in every office, in every company, every day that can keep you from finally getting that new product launched, finally fixing those old bugs, finally leaving work at a reasonable hour. They might be managers who treat whims like emergencies. They might be a CTO's sudden urge to put in for an award. A design tweak at the request of the CEO's best friend. They can even be the guy down the hall who uses his daily breaks as a reason to wander around and make sure everyone else is having a break too. Distractions come in all shapes and sizes.

Not one of them matters.

Projects are sprints. Product design and management is a *marathon*. Relax. Panic and frustration will not make it happen any sooner. It certainly will not make it any more enjoyable.

See past this stuff. Keep your eyes on the long term. That kind of tunnel vision will drive you to get things done. And getting things done is a leadership skill *everyone* wants.

▶ Speaking Up

A funny thing happens to people when they get jobs. They start worrying about keeping them.

No matter how smart they were before they got the job, no matter the reason someone decided to hire them, over time, the politics and constraints and slow decisions of multi-team, multi-stakeholder efforts beat them down and turn them into slow-moving, inhibited, cautious versions of their former selves. Ambition leaves their bodies. Risk and audacity and passion get left for the consultants.

The same people who got so excited about web design that they went to school for it, did it in their spare time, built websites for their neighbors and for local shops for free, and geeked out on every new article and trend and code framework to come along—they crawl into themselves and become agreeable, risk-averse clock-watchers with hardly a pulse.

I'm using strong words here because this trend drives me nuts. I'm betting it drives you nuts too. Maybe this trend has even gotten to *you*.

As a consultant, I'm often hired by people who expect me to do big things in a very short time. They don't have months. They don't always have *weeks*. It's possible I'm picking on slow corporate design because I never get to work that way, but I don't think so. I hear enough people complain about how long it takes to get anything done that I believe a *lot* of people wish they could act like a consultant.

On the flip side of this are the managers. No matter how smart and talented and knowledgeable a person was in the interview, that person's job is now to slow down and dip their toes in the water of a project rather than take charge of it.

Don't let it happen. They're not slowing you down because they want you to be slow. They're doing it because corporations rarely have a sense of urgency. If you want to step up and get things done, *do it*.

Someone hired you, presumably, because you know things. Yet for some reason, the second you got hired, you stopped asserting your knowledge, your passion, your care. You started being afraid. You started worrying about your job instead of your work.

Well, guess what.

It's your job to know when something is bad, and to be able to say so. Assuming you are able to back up your arguments—assuming you *can* demonstrate that you know what you're doing—your job is to do exactly that.

Refuse to play along with bad ideas. Refuse to stop voicing your concerns, your ambitions, your evidence, your knowledge. Your passion for UX got you here. If they don't want it now that they're paying for it, get out. Refuse to work in a place that refuses to consider sound arguments formed by someone who cares deeply for them. If something is bad, and you can back up your opinion with insight, you need to be able to speak up. If you can't, find someplace you can.

Speaking up will make your product better. It'll make your company better. Neglect this, and you're doing only half the job you should be.

That Said

A disclaimer:

If you're new to the profession, backing up your arguments will be tougher for you. You're also less likely to be able to see the complete picture (it's always a much bigger picture than you think). Stick around long enough to get some valuable experience before you start asserting yourself too much. Trying to claim a leadership role before you're ready can damage your reputation before you even get going. Earn it over time.

You'll see when it happens too. It's when people start coming to you instead of the other way around. When you're the go-to person, you're ready to lead.

▶ Taking Criticism

Because I write a lot, I sometimes to go to writers' group meetings. Many of them work in a similar way. People take over a room in a coffeehouse or library or someplace else and then split off into small groups. If you have a piece you'd like to read and have critiqued, you wait until it's your turn and then hand out copies of the writing so everyone can read along while you read aloud. When you're finished reading, each person in the group, one by one, gives you notes on the piece—what's working well, what's not, ideas to consider. While this is happening, you listen and take notes or just absorb. If they have questions, you answer them. Do with the advice what you will, but you came here to get it, so here you go. (This might sound intimidating, but most people there are struggling just as much as you are, even when they're really good.)

On one recent Wednesday night, I noticed that a gentleman whose work I really like was answering a lot of questions. I didn't think anything of it until after a few minutes, when I realized how much more he was answering than the others were asking. Their questions—and this is relatively common in critiques—were gentle ways of pointing out their concerns. Rather than say outright, "I'm having trouble with this particular detail," people tend to disguise the blow in the form of a question. Did you mean for this teenage girl character to sound like an adult? Why do you sometimes explain what a character said rather than using straight dialogue?

They often do this, it seems, for the same reason users blame themselves for making mistakes while using a web app: They think it's their fault for not understanding how the thing works. *Oh,* they say, *I wasn't sure if you meant it that way or not.*

No matter the answer, the people playing critic are doing something important. They're telling you something has concerned them. It's tripped them up somehow.

The gentleman being critiqued that night was working pretty hard to address their questions. *Yes, I meant for her to sound older. I sometimes ditch the straight dialogue because I like to mix things up a little.*

What he *wasn't* doing was listening. He was taking their questions as questions, not as signs of their concern. Something about the dialogue was bothering people. Several readers asked about it. Instead of recognizing this, the writer answered their questions and talked about the character and what he meant here and what was coming next and what happened before and here's why this girl sounds like an adult and here's what she means by this and that and this joke would totally make sense if you'd read the previous chapter.

It reminded me of a whole bunch of conversations I've had with developers and designers over the years. *Why does clicking this button cause this thing to happen? What does this label mean? What happens when you click over here?*

Far more often than not, when you ask questions about a design, you get answers. *Here's what I meant* answers. *That happens because of this other thing* answers. You get answers that explain system constraints, technological issues, bugs, directives from the product manager, you name it. What you don't usually get are responses like, *You know, that's a good point. We should take another look at how we're handling that.*

When it was my turn to comment on the writer's work, I reminded him how much I like his work in general, and that even on his worst day, he's a solid and competent storyteller with great timing and pace and skill. Then I said, "But I'm concerned with how you're reacting to the questions people have asked tonight. Right now, you have the benefit of being able to explain to people what you intend and answer their questions. But when you put this work out into the world, you won't have the liberty of standing over every reader's shoulder to explain what you meant and why you did it this way or that way. They'll have to be able to figure it all out themselves. Your writing will have to be self-evident."

So many times during projects, I've paraphrased the same Neil Gaiman quote: *When a user says something is bothering them, they're almost always right. When a user prescribes a solution, they're almost always wrong.*

The first half of that quote is what applies most here. The other people in the group were indicating that something was bothering them. And they were right to do so. It's not up to the writer to decide if something is good or not; it's up to the reader.

Criticism has a couple of key components.

First, you have to hear the criticism.

A question isn't always a question. Sometimes it's a concern dressed up like a gentle, sweet grandmother with a box of chocolates in her hand. Don't be fooled. If the person asking the question doesn't understand your intention, or the effect of an action in a task flow, or the meaning of a button label, you have cause for concern. Don't just answer the question. Ask counter questions to see what's tripping them up.

Second, you have to be able to accept the criticism with grace.

When you critique others, you don't want a lot of resistance. You want people to keep their heart rates in check long enough to think through what you're telling them and to consider that you might have a point.

Just as you need to be able to criticize, others need to be able to criticize you.

Don't look at the team as a collection of critics. Look at it as a collection of eyes and brains you don't have.

Don't be the person who shoots down any feedback that doesn't go your way. You need people to see the problems in your work. Other people need to trust that you can handle objection. Take criticism well. Because you expect others to do the same.

▶ Being Collaborative

This is a tricky subject.

Loads and loads of people will tell you collaboration is a good thing. And they're right. It is. But only under certain circumstances. Other times, it can be terrible. Especially when it requires compromise.

First, think about collaboration.

A study performed by a management professor at the Wharton School of the University of Pennsylvania and reported on by *Time* magazine (http:// business.time.com/2012/01/19/the-unexpected-costs-of-collaboration) showed that larger teams perform better than small teams despite the fact that individuals on small teams perform better than individuals on large teams. The theory is this: On large teams, people don't know each other as well. When a person on a large team needs help or additional information, he or she is less likely to know who to talk to. But because a larger team has more people on it, it will perform better than the small team overall. An individual on a small team, on the other hand, is more likely to know who to go to for extra information. He or she is also more likely to have a better relationship with that person, because they've worked together more closely than they would on a larger team.

It's a solid argument for collaboration. Basically, in a small, well-run group, you can each benefit from everyone else's knowledge and talent. Small teams have backup skill, overlapping know-how, people with specialties you don't have yourself. As I've stated, individuals can't think of everything. Small groups of people, with their close working relationships and their innate knowledge of who knows what and who's good at what, will invariably make individuals better than they could be on their own. It's a win for everyone.

But not always.

(Warning: You're probably not going to like this.)

Collaboration is really only great when everyone on the team has a pretty stock level of know-how and talent. In those cases, they can help each other out in all sorts of wonderful ways. When a designer is clearly loaded up with talent and drive and smarts, however, that person alone can do way more for a project than a team of lesser designers.

Sorry. It's just true.

(Jeff Stibel once wrote about this for *Harvard Business Review*: https:// hbr.org/2011/06/why-a-great-individual-is-bett.)

A lone designer with extensive experience and reliably good instincts and who can mentally juggle the big picture while simultaneously being able to spot low-level problems from a mile away and consistently see five steps ahead is simply worth more than three people who fall below that mark. Add good communication skills to that (and I don't see how they couldn't be a good communicator with such design talent) and good leadership traits, and you've got yourself a rock star.

However.

Even if you are that person, collaboration can be useful. If not for design purposes, then for political purposes.

The truth is, pretty much no one wants to be excluded from a project because the rock star on the team doesn't need to collaborate. And if you want your whole team to look good (and you do), no single person can stand out as the lone master. Maybe you work better alone. Maybe you *are* better alone. But for the whole team to become relied on, and to keep yourself from being the most interrupted person in the office, collaboration is a good idea.

There are more reasons.

Good ideas are born everywhere. They can come from the least likely places. They can come from the *most* likely places. But they can show up only if people are around to have them. So although being *really good at your job* can make you more capable than a team of lesser designers, logically, at least, there's still a benefit to be had.

Second, genius designers don't operate in a vacuum. They pull ideas and inspiration and insight from multiple sources all the time.

Besides all that, collaborating is often fun. Design can be a lonely business. If you have the chance to bounce ideas off other people, take it. Even if the ideas to come out of it rarely surprise you, they will *sometimes* surprise you. That alone makes collaboration worth trying.

And no one around you will ever trust a loner's design effort as much as they'll trust one they were involved in. If you want to lead, don't ignore the team. Put the team to use. You'll all be better off for it.

Defining "Well-Run"

A "well-run" group, by the way, is one with a clear leader—whose job is to make the final decision—and at least one devil's advocate, whose job is to poke holes in ideas and force people to back them up and think through them completely.

Well-run groups are also limited to as few voices as possible—only those most crucial to the key decisions. Your job is to collect and listen to and consider opinions, but also to remember that there's a gigantic difference between opinion and insight, and that the time it takes to consider too many opinions will keep you from putting any of your insights to work.

▶ Hiring Well

Here's one for the hiring managers. If you are one, read on. If not, you may still benefit from it.

Earlier, I described a guy I interviewed once who said he knows how to scream and wave his arms around to convince people to listen to him. I may not have hired him, but once, someone else just as unqualified did in fact manage to slip through the interview process.

Let's call him Warren.

During the interview, Warren presented himself well. He showed slides of projects he'd worked on. He spoke well. He was able to reference various sources for his continuing self-education (in those days, there was no such thing as a college degree in web design). He had a great demeanor and a willingness to learn and take on challenges. All that good stuff you want in a new hire.

But then.

Once he joined the team, it didn't take long to see how wrong I'd been about him. He didn't seem to have any real design experience at all. When I asked him to sketch out designs, he'd invariably come back with a stack of excruciatingly naïve and oversimplified ideas.

Since he'd said during the interview that he had some experience with usability testing, I asked him to run a round of test sessions for another project I'd been working on. Then I talked him through how to write a test plan. And how to find participants. And how to book the testing lab. How to use the testing software. How to do pretty much everything else involved in a usability test. On the day of the test, I ended up coaching him through how to moderate a test. When the sessions were over, I showed him to analyze the data and calculate ratings. I showed him what information should go in the report so we could communicate the findings to the management team.

It just went on and on. I'd been duped. Hard. This guy knew next to nothing—little enough that I spent much of my time showing him how to spend his.

To this day, I don't know what I missed during that interview that should've been the golden tipoff that Warren would be a bad hire. But since then, I assure you, I've been much more thorough about my hiring decisions.

I start with deciding what's really important to me in a team member. At the very minimum, it's going to be someone who can get through a range of design activities, and some ability to build a rapport with everyone else involved in design efforts. According to Christina Wodtke:

> **With startups and small companies it's going to be one person who has at least a cognizance about [UX skills], even if they can't actually do all of them particularly well yet. Then you've got the soft skill pieces. With only one person, you could say soft skills are unimportant, but that'd be a huge mistake. Because if you** are **the design team—the design team of one—it means you actually have to talk to a bunch of different people who have different mental models about the world. You're going to have to hang out with engineers, who see the world one way, and product managers, who see the world another way, and marketing, who sees the world another way. You're probably going to hang out with the CEO a lot in a small company. You have to actually have a feeling for what the funding is like and will mean to the choices that you're making.**

Basically, you have to be able to communicate in all directions, no matter what skill set or set of priorities a person has. If you're on a small team, or a lone designer in a team of people with other skills, it's up to you to make UX efforts work. Your abilities beyond design—the ones I've talked about throughout this book—are going to be *crucial* to your success.

Jared Spool had some thoughts on this as well:

> *The key thing is soft skills. The problem we see, and what the hiring managers have told us, is that people do not know how to come out of these [degree] programs. They don't know how to present their work, or how to critique, or how to facilitate some sort of group design session. In fact, they don't even know how to write an email, or how to even sit in a meeting without it looking and feeling like it's killing them.*

College, Jared went on to say, teaches people that if you pay attention and work for an hour or 90 minutes, you can go play Frisbee.

There's a lot more to design than Frisbee.

I'm not saying you should avoid college grads altogether. But I am saying you should screen your candidates carefully.

Like so.

Review the Portfolio

Don't just look at it. Have the candidate talk through it. Ask them to explain what they did on the project, what the project goals were, why, how they approached it, and what the outcomes were. If a person can't talk about these aspects of a design effort, either they weren't doing design or they weren't actually involved in making decisions. They may have done what they were supposed to do, but they weren't leading the charge by any means.

Google

Sure, it's questionable whether or not people should be judged by what they've left online, but if you're interviewing a designer, you're interviewing someone who practically lives online. Someone who has opinions about other design work and articles, and who latches on to things that appeal to their designer instincts. Ignore their Facebook profiles. But go find their comments on *Smashing Magazine* pieces. Go find their LinkedIn profiles. Go find their portfolio website (practically every employed designer I've met has had one). Find out how they explain their work, how they think, what they like. You can learn a lot about a person through the breadcrumbs they've left behind them.

Let Them Talk

Earlier, I said to look for the person asking all the questions. This works only if the person is allowed to ask them. So whatever you walk into the interview room wanting to know, be sure to leave plenty of time for the conversation to go other ways. Besides giving the candidate time to interview *you* and see if the company is a good fit, it gives you an out if you know the interview is going badly. You haven't locked yourself into an hour's worth of questions.

When they do talk, take notes. What subjects come up more than others? What are the person's favorite sources for design education? You're going to be interviewing several people. The gut feeling you have tomorrow morning means a lot—really—but anything you can do to trigger distinct memories and back up that gut feeling is a good thing. Especially if you need someone else's approval for the hire.

Contract Them

I have a friend who works for a city government. The hiring process for the city involves a 20-minute initial interview, wherein you are asked the same nine questions as every other applicant and are expected to be able to answer all of them in the allotted time. If you get through that, you're invited back for a 30-minute version, with a total of 11 questions. If you're offered a job, you can be fired for a variety of reasons within the first six months. So they hire you based on almost nothing, and can drop you any time after that. It's essentially a six-month contract meant to look like a permanent job. It's not safe. It just *looks* safe.

Strangely, it's not that far off from the ridiculousness of most web company interview processes. Except for the giant companies, who tend to rely on all-day pressure-fests wherein you meet 20 different people and give a presentation and all kinds of other things, most web companies I've seen interview their candidates over an hour or two. After that, the person is employed. If it turns out to be a bad situation, they can be fired at any time, for pretty much any reason.

Why more people don't mitigate this risk is beyond me.

The absolute best way to see how someone works and how good they are is to work with them on an actual project. So pay them to work with you. Pick a tiny project, or pull them in to help out on a small piece of a project, and see how you do together.

This way, you're not hiring a permanent person you then have to fire three months later. And the designer isn't accepting a job that's really as insecure as could be and based on very little information.

Look for Unicorns

Not everyone will be good at a bunch of things. But anyone you hire at this point should at least be more than one thing. Unless you need a specialist, make sure the person on the other side of the interview table is a generalist in some form.

UX professionals are not graphic designers alone. Or content strategists alone. Or anything else alone. They're people with broad skills and at least one specialty and a lot of passion for figuring out the whole problem and all its effects.

They don't pick colors; they ask questions to sort out how and when and why to use which color. They don't devise layouts; they ask questions to determine relevance, priority, meaning. They don't wait to be told what to do; they lead. If you are interviewing a UX person and *you* are the one asking all the questions, call it off. This is not the UX person you're looking for.

Craft your questions and gear your conversations toward finding out what kind of designer the person in front of you is going to be.

▶ Offering Solutions Instead of Complaints

Earlier, I described the trajectory of a typical designer's career—starting by complaining about bad design and eventually working your way into the ability to make change happen.

Imagine a leader who hadn't done that.

A colleague of mine once had a boss like this. She insisted on reviewing everyone's work, and when she did, the majority of her comments were on what was wrong with a deliverable. She did not say how to fix it, provide any guidelines, or even suggest that a problem *could* be fixed. Her management style, it seemed, was to complain and move on.

Over time, the picture I've pieced together of this person is this:

Prior to becoming a business owner, she had reached a point in her career at which she was relatively capable at her profession. Possibly even *good*. But then she found herself in a position where she couldn't grow anymore. Rather than believing there was more to learn, she assumed she'd learned all she could. (And who knows. Maybe she had.) At this point, she started her own company, where she promptly hired people to do the work she used to do herself and became more concerned with the work of running a business.

Then the business changed. It kept advancing. New rules. New regulations. New policies. The clients evolved, and the professionals working for them evolved.

At some point, my colleague's boss fell behind. She went from Conscious Competence (presumably) to Unconscious Incompetence. She just didn't acknowledge that fact. Instead, she continued assuming she was every bit as capable as she was back when she started the company.

Ten years went by like that.

Her employees—who left the company and were replaced more frequently than at a fast food joint—spent most of their time having their work reviewed and approved by someone whose only ability was to complain. Solving problems was a skill she no longer held.

If you ever find yourself complaining more than contributing, take a vacation. Think through your career choice. Consider whether or not you're still in the right place. If you think you are, choose a new plan for how to be good at it.

No one likes a complainer. Teams need solutions. Leaders bring them.

▶ Giving Credit Away

I used to work with a code-hoarder. You know the type. He's the one who thinks job security is the result of cryptic naming conventions for variables and functions. If he's the only one who can explain it, he surmised, then no one could rob him of his precious programming genius and everyone else would have to come to him. They couldn't fire him, either. They'd be lost trying to crack his secrets.

It was around the same time someone else told me how she was managing to get so much done at work at a different company. She said that although she was new there, she'd been getting all kinds of things approved by giving credit to people around her for their ideas and their contributions. She'd been letting her own credit go in lieu of making things happen. She said, "It's amazing what you can get done when you don't care who gets credit."

I suddenly wanted another job.

The code-hoarder didn't last. When the buyout came and the new overlords took over, code-hoarder was in the first round of layoffs. No one likes a code-hoarder.

Since then I've been giving credit away like it's free. And yes, it does occasionally help get things done. When one person really likes so-and-so and thinks so-and-so's idea is good, you let so-and-so have the credit even when the idea is yours and, prior to five minutes ago, you were the only one who cared about it. No one will remember whose idea it was in three weeks. What they'll remember is that you've gotten a whole lot done in that time.

But that's not why I do it.

I learned something else about credit after I started giving it away. I learned that it makes other people look good, and that when those people are all on your team, your whole team looks good. And this can only have positive effects.

And one other thing.

When you give credit away, people feel appreciated. When they feel appreciated, they get along better, they have better ideas, they appreciate the people around them more, and then they, in turn, *give credit to other people*. It's nutty, I know. But give credit away a few times, and you soon find yourself with a whole bunch of credit-giving happy people who work well together. Insanity.

And one more thing.

They turn around and give credit back to you for all sorts of things. Like being a great leader. Like being a positive force on the team. Like being a person who gets things done.

It just turns into this long, beautiful love-fest.

It might seem counterintuitive, but I swear by it. It creates a culture of self-lessness. It creates an environment of mutual support and respect. It results in a team full of people who are respected and revered for their collaborative natures and their willingness to help each other out.

Build a reputation for your team rather than yourself. Care more about getting it right than putting your name on it.

When it's time for dishing out credit, don't worry. You'll get yours.

▶ Teaching Them to Teach

Way back in the beginning of this book, I mentioned that I was once temporarily involved in the creation of a design curriculum. Since then, I've also spoken at a bunch of web conferences. The thing I didn't see in the curriculum, I also didn't see at the conferences: sessions about persuading people of your ideas. Hence, it took me a long time to even realize this was a skill. I just wondered a lot why people had such trouble getting their bosses to agree with them. To get themselves into concept meetings. I wondered why so many people asked how to go about selling design to stakeholders.

When I talked about this with Jared Spool, he said he's noticed that a few conferences have tried it. Usually, though, it's been taught in separate workshops that had a separate cost, and that this may not have been the best strategy. It's expensive for a company to send its employees to a conference. Those four-hour or whole-day workshops cost even more. And for a person to attend a workshop on soft skills such as persuasion, a couple of big things have to happen before even considering the expense:

First, a person has to be self-aware enough to know he's bad at the soft skill in question and want to improve on it. And that person needs to be brave enough to say to his boss, "Hey, I want to take this workshop so I can get better at convincing you of things. And I'd like for you to pay for it. Oh, and I can't come into work that day. Cool? Thanks."

Next, that person's boss has to agree on the value of the workshop. She has to agree that the designer is weak in that area—weak enough to warrant a budget adjustment, and possibly a conversation with someone higher up to get it adjusted.

It's just not the kind of conversation that happens every day.

(If sessions on soft skills were already part of the conference lineup, that'd be a different story. Then you could go without any awkwardness.)

As I've noted earlier in this book, much of your job as a UX professional is not about designing but about selling your ideas. It's about convincing people your recommendations are merited and considered and probably right (based on your experience and your research, which you will be able to show as part of your pitch).

This is also true of everyone else on your UX team.

And since that's true, and since you're unlikely to end up in a conference workshop about it, it's important to think about other ways to get that information out to the rest of your team. Teach them to teach.

One way is to interrupt your internal brown bag tech lunches with a talk on a particular soft skill. Any of the skills talked about in this book, for example.

You could work some tips into your everyday conversations. When another designer complains about being unable to get past an obstacle.

You could make it a personal policy to always educate those around you by explaining why you made the recommendations you did.

You could leave copies of this book lying around the office.

It's entirely possible the people around you don't even know they need to get better at persuading people of their ideas. Maybe they don't know how to lead. Maybe they think that until they're in the right chair, their job is to follow. Maybe they don't know all the benefits of explaining the rationale behind their ideas.

If you are part of a team, no matter which role you're in, make it an absolute priority to help the other people on the team learn to sell their ideas. Make sure they know how to make their case, and that they need to in the first place.

If you can't convince, you can't succeed. And neither can they.

▶ Managing Things Away from People

Years ago, Seth Godin wrote a couple-of-hundred-word blog post describing his belief that he doesn't have a staff, he works *for* his staff. They're the ones doing all the work. His job is to get out of their way.

During a project once, I had a side conversation with a project leader. I said, "There are exactly two kinds of managers." To which he said, "And only two kinds." He knew what I meant, which is that there are managers who get in your way, and leaders who get out of it.

I've had plenty of experience with both. One is always better (the one who gets out of the way).

There are a lot of perspectives on the difference between management and leadership. They show up in books, in web articles, in seminars. The debate isn't all that useful. What *is* useful is to understand the difference between what *should* be managed and what *gets* managed. They are usually very different things.

What usually *gets* managed is people. Managers think they are being paid to organize and to delegate and to track. This is a myth. And believing it is a detriment to productivity.

People want to do good work. It's human nature. They want to feel proud of their effort. If it seems like they don't, it's usually because they think their current situation prevents them from doing so and have become resigned to that idea, because your version of "good" and theirs have different definitions, or because you are at different points on the spectrum with regard to your ability to evaluate what "good" means. (In any case, addressing the underlying problem is the only effective way to deal with it.) It's not because they want to do bad work.

Besides this, we in the web industry have a distinct advantage that some other industries might not have: *We work in the web industry.*

People who join the web industry do it with their whole selves. They become absolute freaks for this work. They love it. They eat it for breakfast. You don't need to *manage* people in the web industry. You need to manage things *away* from people in the web industry. If you are a manager of some kind, in other words, your job is not to tell people what to do, but to keep things out of their way so that they can do what they already want to do.

I took Seth's blog post to heart. I've had plenty of bad days on projects led by people who wanted to micro-manage and run every detail. When I've run teams, my goal has never been to delegate and dictate. It's been to keep problems and distractions and politics off the desks of my team. They are, as Seth pointed out, the people who are doing the work. I'm not there to be a designer, or a content strategist, or a usability test moderator. I'm there to help the people on my team be those things.

If you are in charge, try to focus on managing things away from people instead of managing people. Lead by example. Mentor rather than manage.

▶ Creating Opportunities for Others

Back in Chapter 2, I said that being replaceable means you're doing a job that few designers do but that they all should: helping others on your team become as well-rounded as you are. Here's what that looks like in reality.

I once had a junior designer on my team who desperately wanted to do more strategy work. He'd told me so at least three times while the team was in the midst of a Herculean effort to rid itself of technical debt. He was at his least challenged, design-wise. He wanted to push himself.

I understood. This isn't what any of us had signed up for. I was just as eager to get back to doing rather than *re*doing.

A couple of weeks later, a project I'd been pushing for came to fruition. It was something I had been planning for a few weeks and had spent a good amount of time convincing the relevant stakeholders to take on. It was a project I really wanted to work on myself.

Strategy came first. My wheelhouse. My favorite part. But something was gnawing at me.

This designer was really talented. He showed up every day. He slogged through the projects that had kept us all from any kind of forward motion. He did stellar work no matter how tedious the project. From the moment I'd joined the company, I'd wanted to see how far he could go, and here he was, stuck in the mud, not getting anywhere. He wanted very much to do more strategic work, and I very much wanted to give him the chance.

I had to do it. I gave the project to him. I told him I'd be there for guidance and to answer questions if he needed, but that the project was all his.

Secretly, I also committed to asking him loads of questions along the way that would allude to the kinds of things he should be thinking about. But I swore to myself I would give him some distance. Remember: Good ideas come from all kinds of places. We all needed to see what he could do, most of all him. He needed room to step out. To step up.

And so he did.

He did great work on that project. He proved himself to a bunch of people in a bunch of ways. And he learned some things in the process that enabled me to go to him later as a strategic thinker.

Again, people in the web industry already want to do great work. They want to learn more, take on more, build more, design more, ship more. They're hungry.

So feed them.

When someone wants the chance to improve at something, find ways to let them. The next time a project comes up that appeals to that person, hand it off, even if you really want to do it yourself. Nine times out of ten, that person will step up. And both of you will be better off for it.

Even if you're not in the position to decide which people belong to which projects, you can always find little ways to involve others. If they're interested in the thing you're working on, invite them over to see what you can do together.

A little advice, though, if you're on the other side of this scenario—if you *are* the person who wants more opportunities: Do something to earn them.

I once invited onto a project of mine a designer who'd been pretty well known for his talents. He had worked at a local agency for a long time and had recently gone out on his own to become a consultant. He'd said to me a few weeks earlier that he, too, wanted to get more into strategic work. So when a project popped up that would involve a lot of it, I asked him to join the client and me for a two-day kickoff session. He accepted. We holed up for a couple of days in a conference room and cranked out a bunch of ideas, and then planned to refine them over the next week or so. During those two days, he was great. He was full of ideas, we worked well together, the client liked him, and we got a lot done. His next job was to go create a more complete version of the strategy, make sure our initial design ideas supported it, and put together some more refined screens. We'd have a meeting about it the next Monday.

He never showed up to the meeting on Monday. And days later, when we pressed to see what he'd done, he sent us a digital version of a single sketch we'd done on a whiteboard the week earlier.

I haven't invited him into a project since. I'm sure you can see why.

If you want people to include you, be there when the invitation comes. Be present. Be reliable. Be engaged. The only way to get better is to drown a little bit. Be ready to jump in the pool.

▶ Choosing Teams Over Individuals

That giant company I worked with—the one with the middle manager who spent three weeks on a project with no strategy, the one the former CEO then dismantled in 20 minutes flat—they had a big problem to solve outside of petty managers. The company had 20 or 30 different products in its portfolio, and until a year or so earlier, they'd had no centralized design team.

This company had a ton of designers. Every product team had at least one designer assigned to it. Some had several. Then someone with a directorial perspective thought to try to unify the company's product designs by bringing together all those designers and developing design standards to be used throughout the company. Each product would have its own challenges, of course, and its own idiosyncrasies, but those distinctions could be fed back into the larger set of standards and be made available for other special cases like them. Eventually, customers using multiple products could rely on coherent, learnable interfaces that always felt familiar after using just one of the others.

The Central Design team was born.

The director vacuumed up some of the best people from other places in the company, hired a few seasoned veterans from outside, got to work studying the similarities and differences and standards and exceptions to product design throughout the company, and started turning them into a core knowledge base for designers on every product team.

This would take a long time, of course. And it would be really tough to do. Most companies recognize this opportunity to centralize design standards much earlier—long before they find themselves with 20 different products to wrangle. But the past is past.

I learned about the team a year into the process. The director said they'd been making headway. They'd earned the respect of the product managers for several of the bigger products, and she felt like the team was gaining enough momentum that it could soon reach a tipping point. They'd get to companywide adoption soon enough.

Only whenever I mentioned Central Design to people I worked with at the company, no one seemed to have heard of it. If they had heard of it, they said so with a vague "I don't know that much about it" sort of reply that came complete with a shoulder shrug.

They weren't getting their names out there as much as they thought.

I wasn't around long enough to try to help further that cause, but I knew the feeling. I'd had to do the same thing at a previous company, albeit a much smaller one. It got me thinking. Not only about what I'd done before myself, but about what kinds of things this company could do.

My answer?

All of it. Do *everything* in this chapter.

Rather than let the rock stars get all the recognition, lift up your whole team. Teach them to teach others. Give credit away. Help people stay calm in the face of obstacles so that the team's reputation remains positive. Offer solutions instead of complaints. Educate.

Do it all.

If you focus on making the whole team great, the whole team will become known as a reliably credible resource. The team itself will bond more when cooperation rather than contention is the default, and the company as a whole will benefit from it every day.

Stay steadfast to the ideas in this chapter—this book—and when it comes time for credit to be passed around, you'll get your credit.

You'll get your credit.

9

Learning

Ten thousand hours. That's what Malcolm Gladwell says in his book *Blink*. It takes 10,000 hours to move from what Harry Max calls Unconscious Incompetence to Mastery.

It's a long road. An overwhelming road.

At 40 hours a week for 52 weeks, that's 4.8 years' worth of office work. And let's be real here: You take vacations, you take holidays, you have a fake cold once in a while, you're really looking at probably 48 weeks over a year. That puts you at 5.2 years to hit your 10,000 hours. And that's if your job description is relatively tightly scoped. If you're a generalist, it will take much longer to master a single skill, because you'll spend much less time developing that skill alone.

If you're the kind who likes to go slow, learn at your own pace, check out after 40 hours, fine. Nothing says you need to bolt your way into Mastery. Web design isn't the Olympics. You can cruise along for a while at your most mediocre level and get by just fine. Talent and ambition abound in this industry. Those other people, the ones who *have* become masters, will surely help you along at your leisure.

But it'll take you longer than 10,000 hours to get to Mastery. Because it takes more than just 10,000 hours; it takes 10,000 *feverish* hours. Hours when you can't get the work out of your head. Hours when you *burn* to know more, burn to do more.

If you don't burn for it, you're in the wrong business. If you don't burn for it, your entire career will feel like work. The kind your parents did. The kind that burned them out rather than lighting them on fire.

If you burn for it, it's not work. If you burn for it, you'll excel at it. You'll thrive because of it. You'll look up from your laptop once a year and write a list of all the things you've done and wonder how on earth you did it all. You won't notice how much you're accomplishing along the way because you'll be focused on the love of it rather than the achievement. You're not stacking up credentials, you're having fun.

If you burn for the work, the credentials will come. Do what you love and the money follows.

These feverish hours also have to be lived well, pursued for their deepest value. You can perform a menial task for 10,000 hours and become only mildly more proficient at it. Stick to the same kinds of design projects all the time—the kind you're comfortable with, the ones that stay small and manageable—and you'll get to the same place you always were. You can make a career out of it.

That kind your parents had.

If you want to blow past all that, do something awesome once in a while, do something *satisfying*—you'll need more than hours alone. You'll need a mind-set.

▶ How I Learned

When I built my first site in the late '90s, college degrees in web design were several years off from becoming a reality. Educational sources were slim. They were mostly online. (It was a time when people still got their educations almost exclusively in schools, so online education about web design was strangely self-referential.) The websites that taught people how to make websites were pretty great, but they were few and far between, and they spoke not a word about "user experience" or "interaction design." They talked about how to build complicated tables in HTML—yes, tables— to handle all your layout needs. That's about as sophisticated as front-end web design got back then. No psychology. No UX strategy. No research. (All of this, I'm sure, had quite a bit to do with the dot-com crash that occurred shortly thereafter.)

As awful as all that sounds, I think there was a benefit to it. It was tough to learn anything beyond common HTML and JavaScript techniques, so most of our practices had to be invented. We had to try things and be ter-rible at them and learn what didn't work and what did. We had to codify our lessons into methods. We had to teach.

Fighting to gain all this knowledge that would eventually become com-monplace seemed to make people all the more committed to morphing the "passing trend" of the Internet into a profession. Every last person working in the web industry did their work like it was the last day of their lives and work was the only thing that would save them. I think I hit my first 10,000 hours three years in. I worked at work. I worked at home. I did side projects. I did personal projects. Then I chose a specialty and put in another 10,000. At some point, I probably put 5000 hours into *talking* about UX. I couldn't begin to calculate how many hours I've put into writing about it. It's been a busy 16 years. Obsession will do that to you.

Now, you can go to school for web design just as you can to become an accountant. Just pick it as your major, sign up for the classes, learn everything in digestible, 90-minute increments with beer and Frisbee between, and then walk out a few years later with some vague sense of competence.

There are advantages to this ease of access to useful information, of course—I could've gotten a lot more sleep—but something's been lost, I think, along the way.

The fire.

Yes, lots of people still dive in with their whole selves, but that might look different now than it used to. You can go to school thinking you can learn it all there. You can leave school without the fever to learn more. You can leave school not even realizing the first thing you have to do is learn how to get through an entire 40-hour workweek.

Basically, the learning part suffers when you can check in and out of it according to the fall schedule.

When that's a hurdle to start with, there's much less chance you'll learn that Mastery requires a lot more than 40 hours a week, and much less chance you'll pour yourself into the attempt with the fever of a thousand suns.

And much less chance you'll be the leader you want to be.

I'm not suggesting you need to work 80 hours a week for life. I'm the *last* person who would advocate that. But I am suggesting that the fire is *vital* if you want to sustain a career in this profession, even if you only devote a reasonable number of hours per week to it.

▶ Why Learning Matters

How to write a test plan for a usability test and then screen and schedule participants. How to run a kickoff meeting. How to define strategy. How to analyze data and tweak a design based on it. Everything else. It all takes time. And this is without even mentioning the *human psychology* involved in UX. The toughest part. The deepest subject. The richest and most nuanced field of observation.

It's not so likely you'll stumble across the new insights and revelations of a leader until you've at least become relatively comfortable with all the activities and skills you need to get through the typical project—until you can speak the language and know what it all means. Gain some fluency in the ways of UX.

You don't have to be a master of all things UX to become a leader, but it certainly helps to do so in at least one area. Anyone with a passing interest in UX can become mediocre at it. We don't need more mediocrity. Mediocrity is a drag. If you perpetuate the status quo, preach the same ol' standards the experts are trying to push past, you'll do more harm than good to your teammates, especially if you're out in front, leading the team.

If you prove yourself mediocre and happy with that, those who are better and more experienced will resist pulling you into tougher situations.

That strive for greatness is what gets you into the good projects. The good jobs. And ultimately, learning and then sharing those lessons is what pushes the *profession* forward. And if you're doing that, you are most definitely a leader.

In those years when I was swimming in the dark and trying to guess my way through every project, nearly every day was a learning experience. I read everything. I tried everything. I tracked everything.

I worked a lot.

Again, I'm not advocating you slowly kill yourself by stacking up office hours. That just leads to burnout. But I do think it takes more than a few hours a week to get where you want to go. Learning is exponential, and the quicker you do it, the sooner you'll be able to see your own limitations.

A few years ago, I tried out a new form of drumming—the kind taught in a studio with other people who were divided into groups. I've been a drummer my whole life, but this style was brand new to me. For the first year, I thought I was doing well. I was picking it up quickly, and I already had all that musical knowledge to rely on in the first place, so I felt pretty good about my progress. Then I saw myself on video.

It was not a good day.

Despite my awfulness, I got bumped up to the intermediate group. When I did, I continued practicing in the beginner group to get in some extra practice time each week. I immediately realized I was learning a lot more playing twice a week than I was when I played just once. Not just because I was playing twice as often, but because more of the lessons sank in between practices. They stayed fresher in my head. The muscle memory started to build up at a much faster rate.

Soon, I'd moved from the intermediate group to the advanced group, at which time I dropped out of the beginner practices but stayed in the intermediate group. By then, I'd started to realize how hard this new craft was. A year after that, I was invited into the performing group—the one that hopped up onto public stages on a regular basis and played for large groups of people. By then, I knew how bad I really was compared to a professional. And I learned more then than I ever had.

Let me say that again.

I learned more in the performing group than I ever had before.

It wasn't exclusively *because* I was in the performing group. It was because by the time I'd joined that group, I'd consistently been playing two or three times a week for a couple of years with better and better players, on more and more sophisticated music. By the time I'd gotten as far as I could go within this particular studio, I knew exactly how much further I'd never get unless I were to jump over to a better studio. I could see behind me, when I was truly terrible, and I could see ahead to a level I would never reach within my current situation.

You learn better when you do it more frequently. And you gain a better context for your level of understanding and knowledge once you get some serious education behind you and you can see how far you've come.

You have to see what's behind to understand what's ahead. To lead, you have to have followed. Apparently, you also have to have been awful on video at least once.

You have to be willing to be humbled.

▶ Leaving Your Ego Out of It

It's a funny thing, ego.

During my second year in that drumming group, a new player mysteriously appeared one day. He'd called the studio a couple of weeks earlier to say he'd recently relocated from Japan to Phoenix (where I live) to go to school for one year. He wanted to know if he could come play with the group while he was holding temporary residency. The group's director happily invited him to join in. He showed up one day. Then he showed up the next day. During the first week or so, he sat in with almost every group, watching, listening, looking, not saying a word. He stayed hidden in the back corners of the room. He never spoke up, never asked questions. Shy, maybe.

After a few days, the veterans of the studio started to notice that he seemed to be picking up on the music really quickly. He had good form. He had good rhythm. So they asked:

"Have you been playing long?" He said, "Sort of."

"Do you know how to play this drum?" He said, "A little."

"And this one?" He said, "A little."

This was not a man who was comfortable talking about himself.

"What group did you play with in Japan?"

His answer? It turns out he was the founder and lead drummer of a famous drumming group. One of the remarkably few famous drumming groups.

The kind that practiced for hours every day. The kind who lived together and practiced together and ate together. The kind that went on tour for six or eight months of every year and who had played all over the world. He'd started it back in high school. He was 30 years old when we met him. It was his group.

I got to play alongside him once a week for the whole year he was in Phoenix. And here's the funny part.

He never said a word about himself. He never spoke about his group back in Japan. He never outplayed us. He never told stories about playing to crowds of hundreds in the Netherlands or Switzerland or all over North America. He never interrupted anyone. He never said someone was wrong. When we asked him to help, he did, and with as few words as possible.

Compare that behavior to the middle manager from my earlier story who refused to let me on to another project after I'd advocated a new direction for his project.

That's just how it is, isn't it? The guy with the ego has a lot to defend. The guy with *no* ego is the one who keeps learning, keeps teaching, keeps being valuable to himself and those around him.

Leaving your ego at the door is no small feat. But when it comes to learning, and advancing, and listening, it's essential. It's essential to gaining any level of mastery.

If you are at the beginning of your career—anytime before your first 10,000-hour mark, let's say—focus on what's great about having your ego trampled on. It has a lot of benefits. I swear.

Consider a usability test—the first usability test ever done on something you designed.

It was tough, right?

Strangers showed up. They tried to use a design you'd spent a couple of weeks on. Something you were confident about. They stumbled and tripped and got lost. They said out lout how hard a time they were having. And you couldn't believe it. And you went home feeling lousy.

Or the first time you saw data that said people were getting stuck on a page and abandoning a process you were so sure was simple and clear.

And you learned from it.

It can take a long time to teach yourself that it's nothing personal. That it's not about being right or not, or being perfect on the first try. It's about learning.

Design is an experiment. Every last bit of it is an experiment.

Yes, it's a good idea to try to do it as well as you can. No, it's not a good idea to think you've nailed it, and then be horribly disappointed when you find out you didn't. It's an experiment.

Your job is to learn. It's to listen. It's to consider, and include, and collaborate, and investigate, and tweak, and revise, and check, and *learn*.

Let your ego be crushed. Let it stay that way.

A woman in the performing group I played in told me once that she had a goal for the upcoming year. It was startlingly simple but would be insanely hard to achieve.

Her goal was to finally give up her ego once and for all.

She was pretty great at it already. She's always been known for being the most joyful person in the room. She dances. She makes jokes. She laughs hysterically—sometimes so hard that we wonder if she's stopped breathing altogether. She's gleefully self-deprecating.

Part of her pursuit to give up her ego, she once told me, meant never dealing with people in frustration. She dealt with them by asking, "What can I learn from this person?"

She's mastered the art of learning. And everyone around her knows what they've learned from her: You can always improve.

Drown a Little Every Day

Another big part of relinquishing your ego in a career context involves taking on the kinds of projects and jobs that make you feel a little queasy.

At the time of the interview for my very first web design job, I had about a week's worth of skill. I spent an afternoon the week earlier taking in as much as I could about the ways of HTML, I built a little website, and then I replied to a job listing in the newspaper. Web design jobs were listed in newspapers back then.

During the next job, I hand-coded a commerce site composed of hundreds of product pages. At the next one, I was hired to be the office technologist. I was expected to know not only how to construct Flash-based interactive compact disc business cards, but also how to configure the telephony system and fix the laser printer. Later on, I became a courseware designer at an eLearning company. Then a programmer at another one. Then a designer tasked with starting a team and disrupting a massive programming department for a leading software company.

During the first 10 years of my career, I think I was in over my head about 90 percent of the time I was breathing. And don't get me wrong here—it's stressful, and harrowing, and anxiety-riddled.

But it's also a lot of fun. And the payoffs have been great. The insights I've gotten about human psychology, the amazing people I've been able to work with in that time, all the projects that came to life and then changed and then died only to be born again and turned into something else. If you like it when things get stale, the web business is not for you. If you're not nervous about whether you can pull something off, then you're not trying hard enough. If you're not naturally curious, you may sustain a career for a while, but it won't be the wild ride it could be. It won't be fun.

Always go for the job that feels a little out of reach. Always go for the project that feels a little impossible. You have to risk being lousy. Without that risk, you're just doing the same old thing. Without risk, there's no hope for real success. Being lousy is the fun part.

There is simply nothing in the world like being in over your head.

Be dumb. Be awful. Be challenged. It's the only way to get better.

▶ Learning to Succeed, Not to Embrace Failure

Time for a sports metaphor. It had to happen.

When I was a kid, I played Little League baseball for several seasons. During tryouts for the first couple of seasons, my fielding was mediocre and my batting was average at best. I'm not sure I could run very fast either. Because of all this, I got shoved out into the outfield. For two full seasons, I played either left or right field and did almost nothing during the games. Ten-year-olds aren't so great at swinging for the fences. I did a lot of standing around.

When it was my turn to bat, I swung at the air a lot while the ball flew past my head. I never hit a thing. I had a terrible eye.

During practices, I could hit the ball at least once in a while. And it wasn't the coach being nice to me with slow pitches—it was our starting pitcher. Once a week, maybe, I'd swing and the ball would go flying. For whatever reason, during games I just couldn't introduce the ball to my bat to save my life.

I was never going to be a pro baseball player. I accepted it. I just went about the business of crouching in the outfield every time a batter stepped into the box, knowing full well he'd never hit anything my way and that I was only doing it because the coach said to.

Prior to my third season, tryouts went about the same as they had before. Once again, I trudged to my spot in the outfield to practice crouching.

Then, right before the season started, the catcher got sick. The kid had mononucleosis. The kissing disease. After getting over my momentary admiration for the guy, I realized this meant we'd need a new catcher. My coach said the spot was open for tryouts.

I tried out.

I did well.

I got the gig.

And by the time the kid with mono got healthy again, I'd taken his spot, fair and square. I was a better catcher than he was. At every practice and every game, I wrapped myself up in all that catcher's gear, got down behind home plate, and pulled in ball after ball. And I was proud of my new status.

Then, during a game, something *really* strange happened. A white object came flying at me, I heard my bat crack against it, and I watched a baseball fly into the outfield, where I'd spent the previous two seasons. Then it hit the ground. And people shouted, "Run!" And I did. And I was on second base before they threw up their hands and yelled, "Stop!" A few swings by another kid later, and I slid over home plate despite the fact that I was at no risk whatsoever of being tagged out.

The next game, it happened again. And the next. The one after that, I hit a single and was disappointed. Then I went back to doubles.

I got a hit during almost every game that season.

But wait. There's more.

We frequently practiced this wild-pitch play. It was our contingency plan for when the pitcher threw a bad pitch that hit the ground and then bounced off into space where I couldn't see it. My job was to throw my mask off, whip around, find the ball, and grab it before anything bad happened. This wild pitch tended to happen when someone was on third base and the pitcher was nervous. In this situation, it was the pitcher's job to run to home plate so I could toss him the ball and he could tag the guy out.

We practiced it a lot. It was a tough play for twelve-year-olds.

During games, it never worked. Not even my newfound self-esteem could make it work. The ball would go flying, I'd find it, toss it to the pitcher too late, and the play would be over. The other team had their run.

And then one day, it happened. Wild pitch. Mask. Ball flying. Dirt everywhere. I nabbed the ball and whipped around, and for the first time, the pitcher was right where he was supposed to be at the same time I was, and the runner had not yet hit home plate, and I tossed the ball to the pitcher, and he swung his glove down to tag the runner, who was now in a full slide, on the ankle.

Out.

Then came the cheering. Then came the coach, running onto the field with a group of uniformed kids behind him, screaming and clapping. Then came the back-patting. The congratulations. We may as well have won a championship that day. Because for once, we'd nailed it. It had taken work and practice and patience, but we'd nailed it.

If you've been in the web industry for any length of time, you've probably heard at least once by now the idea of embracing failure.

I want to talk about this for a minute because it's been plaguing the professional world for a number of years, and it's the stupidest idea you could possibly support.

I don't know who started it, but over the years it's turned into quite the plague. A couple of PhDs once wrote a book about the idea of embracing failure. For a little while, there was a conference called FailCon, which served to promote and celebrate the idea of failing. It closed up when the idea became so prevalent that it no longer needed promotion. Silicon Valley has practically turned the idea of embracing failure into a virtue. (Which I guess isn't so surprising when you consider how frequently businesses there fail.) People raise their kids now to get participation trophies. Success isn't the important part, they seem to say. It's showing up. It's trying. Sometimes people cite Einstein as support for the idea by using his quote, "I have not failed. I've just found 10,000 ways that won't work." Which is, of course, seriously misguided, because Einstein was literally saying he had *not* failed. Failure certainly wasn't his goal. He was ruling things out on the way to success.

A little Googling uncovered a WikiHow article on *how* to embrace failure. One of the steps is "Stop being sad."

Seriously.

I know. I'm a curmudgeon. But my beef with this ridiculous idea has merit—on several fronts.

First, I concede that this is partly a semantic issue. The people who perpetuate the idea of embracing failure don't mean you should fail. They mean you should push yourself. You should try everything. You should see how far you can go. I get that. But "failure" is a strong and terrible word.

It describes a *lack* of success. The state of *not functioning*. The state of *not* doing something you were supposed to do.

Earlier, I talked about the value of writing well. One guideline in writing is to avoid phrases that express the negative and instead reword them to focus on the positive. Here's an example:

I tried to get through the party looking like I wasn't having too terrible a time.

The positive version of that?

I tried to look like I was having a good time.

Much tidier. It takes less effort to put the words in the affirmative than it does to tongue-twist your way out of the negative. (The previous sentence, by the way, is another fine example of negative phrasing.)

But this is the weakest of my arguments. Here are some stronger ones.

Prophecies Like to Be Self-Fulfilling

Human beings are susceptible to a lot of persuasive tricks. One of them is repetition. Say something over and over again according to a strategy (like the one at http://smallbusiness.chron.com/repetition-persuasive-strategy-26001.html) and people often start to believe it whether it has any merit or not. It's how presidents get elected. It's how wars are started. It's how an entire company can be convinced, rightly so, that *design matters.*

Manipulative? Heck yeah, it's manipulative. Manipulation is a good thing. It's a necessary tool. Call it "persuasion" or "influence" if it makes you more comfortable. Just wrap your brain around it. Treat it well and it will serve you well.

But remember that repetition also reinforces your *own* beliefs. The more you say something, the harder it is to change your own mind about it later. Be careful about what you repeat. You can give gravity to your own bad habits and ideas.

Like failing.

Say it often enough, say it with enough fervor, and you'll think you're doing great every time your soup comes out of the microwave too hot.

Even if you know that the intent is the opposite, the word "failure" sitting in your head all day is self-destructive. Things go wrong in any job, in any career. It's of no use to you to get it into your head that failing is a goal, even if it really means pushing yourself past the known and achievable. Far better to set a goal you *want* to achieve.

Leaders Don't Root for Failure

Consider what leaders do. Rather, what they don't do.

They don't stand on rooftops and shout, "Fail!" They don't revel in the glory of failure. No baseball coach has ever shouted from the dugout that failing was fine as long as you got up and kept going. And certainly no baseball coach has ever run onto the field from the dugout with a team of cheering kids behind him because you hit a foul ball, dropped your bat, and then sprained your ankle.

This doesn't happen. Because leaders don't root for bad ideas. Leaders fend them off.

Failure is a bad mind-set. Besides being inefficient, it focuses on all the wrong things. Psychological studies have shown that negative thinking contributes to stress. Health studies have shown that it contributes to— well, poor health. And while the whole idea of embracing failure seems intended to help people convince themselves of the *upside* of failing, the mere focus on the idea means you're aiming at the wrong goal. You're celebrating all the times the wild-pitch play went south during practice.

Leaders don't do that.

Repeated Failure Gets You Nowhere

Repeated failure doesn't teach you how to succeed. Success teaches you how to succeed.

When startup entrepreneurs succeed once, they are more likely to succeed again. When they fail, however, they are just as likely to fail the next time around as they were the first time. This is what venture capitalists have found to be true, anyway.

Some people believe you can learn as much from failing as you can from succeeding. This is just not true. There are a billion ways to do both, but only one of these outcomes is desirable. You're not trying to learn how to fail. That's absurdly easy to do. There's nothing to learn there. You're trying to learn to succeed.

Fail once and you've learned one way to fail. But succeed once and you've learned at least one way to succeed. And if you learn to succeed one way, your odds go up for learning to do it another way. Because in the process of succeeding, you pick up a few skills necessary for doing it again. You learn how to shift strategies. How to prioritize. How to rethink. How to sit back and stare at the rafters for a minute to reimagine how you'll achieve the goal. You learn how to push through the obstacles. How to align the variables that will give you a positive outcome.

Most of all, you learn that *success is possible*, which is essential to believing it can happen again.

When designers succeed, they take away a lesson. An insight they can apply in other situations later. They can start next time around with something they knew was true once. They can start closer to being correct. When they fail, they frequently learn nothing from the experience. They're just as likely to fail the next time.

On any given day, there are so many different ways to fail that learning one doesn't necessarily mean you're getting any closer to ruling out all the others. Web design has a *ton* of variables. It could take years to rule out all the possibilities and find a method for success. *Years.*

Of course, it doesn't.

Why?

What Exactly Is Success in Web Design Anyway?

Despite all I've said here, success in web design is a nebulous idea at best.

The second you start picking at this idea of embracing failure, it turns to vapor. Because there is no true benchmark for success or failure in business. Sure, you can point to certain companies and call them successes. But you can also point to each one and call them the opposite, often for the very reasons that enable the illusion of success.

Does financial growth indicate success? What if it happened because the company started charging more? Or because it acquired a smaller company and therefore has more revenue despite also having more debt?

Does a spike in user registrations indicate success? What if along with that, more users abandon their accounts after a few months, more than ever before?

How about a "time on page" metric? Does a user who spends a lot of time on a page indicate you've succeeded at keeping their attention? Or does it mean they're stuck and don't know what to do next?

Success and failure can both be the mere effect of which way you're holding the flashlight.

It's not a semantic debate. It's a scope debate. Whether you've succeeded or failed depends on the exactness of the goal and how many other factors you ignore. If what you were trying to do was get an increase in user registrations, and you did that, and you did *not* take into account how long users stick around as customers, then you've succeeded. If you wanted more long-term customers, and you could see after six months that you'd achieved that, even if it meant getting fewer registrations and fewer customers overall, then you've succeeded.

It's also a validity debate. Turn the flashlight one way, you're a success. Turn it another, you've done something else. You can succeed at making money and fail at upholding your ethics. You can succeed at drawing in more customers via a good marketing campaign, but fail in doing it with a good product.

Is success or failure even a valid question in the context of web design?

No. Not really.

People just like to think it is.

Web design is not a matter of practicing the same thing over and over until you finally pull it off. It's a question of trying a million different things until you figure out some combination of variables that seem to be working well enough right now for the goals you have but could probably be done in a better way and probably should very soon.

Success and failure are non-ideas. Stop measuring your work by them.

Measure your work by whether or not it's doing what you hoped in a way that makes you proud. Are the people who use the product happy with it? Do they *like* it?

Do *you* like it?

Dig for a few minutes into any company and you can find something about it that just feels terribly wrong. The longer you work, the older you get, the more adept you become at seeing it. You can stack up tiny wins every single day if you want, but over a long enough timeline, the only measure that matters is whether you feel good about what you did and how you did it.

Do what makes you proud.

▶ Aim for the Breakthrough

If you must put the world into boxes of success and failure, however, then remember my baseball story. And affirmative phrases. And the power of repetition.

The notion of embracing failure promotes the idea of looking forward to the moment you rule something out rather than the moment you finally achieve something. It focuses on steps rather than goals.

For crying out loud, stop doing it. There is little virtue in pursuing failure. There is far more in pursuing the breakthrough.

When you get your ego crushed by a bad outcome, don't call it failure. It's not failure unless you actually fail—a product loses revenue, its funding runs out, the shop closes down. Most of the time, what you're doing is work. Plain ol' work. It's inventing and iterating. It's learning to succeed.

I didn't write this book by first learning how to do it badly. I wrote it by writing it. By whipping off the catcher's mask and finding the ball and tagging the guy out. By swinging the bat. The only acceptable outcome for me was to complete it.

Believe me, I did not embrace the difficulties. There is nothing fun about waking up every morning for months on end knowing that if you get a little behind today, you'll be a lot more behind next week. It is not always easy to be instructive and useful on demand. I pushed past the difficulties. When I was done, I went back over the whole thing and reviewed it and made it better. There was no failure to be found in this process, only forward motion. If you want the project to get done, there is only the doing to worry about.

You will get frazzled. You will get interrupted. You will get distracted and frustrated and anxious. These are not things to embrace. Don't even pay attention to them. Ignore them, look for the outcome you want, and keep going until you reach it. One day, you will tag the guy out. One day, the baseball will fly into center field. *These* are the moments to embrace.

Don't aim for failure. *Aim for the breakthrough.*

You're not failing. You're testing theories. You're validating ideas. You're ruling things out. You're iterating.

You're learning.

So do that. Don't fail. *Learn.*

10

Being Unreasonable

▶ The Advantage of High Standards

▶ Designing for Greatness

The reasonable man adapts himself to the world. The unreasonable one persists in trying to adapt the world to himself. Therefore all progress depends on the unreasonable man.

—*George Bernard Shaw*

Let's say you want to do great work. Let's say you want to craft designs that have positive effects on the people who use them. Designs that make people's lives easier, and better, and more manageable.

You might think that being a reasonable leader is the way to get there. It's not. The reasonable aren't leaders.

As much as we'd all like to work with people who seem consistently reasonable, and though some of us may wish to be viewed by others as reasonable, Shaw was talking about a different kind of reasonableness. He wasn't referring to the kind of person who makes decisions with a calmness. A pleasant demeanor. Someone who gets things done without an enormous spike in blood pressure. Someone who leads without a shark's teeth.

Sure, these may all be good qualities. No one would blame you for wanting them in a mentor, a colleague, a boss. And pursuing this level-headedness for yourself can only work to your advantage.

But Shaw wasn't talking about those qualities. He was talking about the driving force behind those qualities—the force that makes them useful.

Being pleasant is only useful if your pleasantries allow to you to still have an effect. Making decisions with calmness is useful only if those decisions have been based on considered evidence. Getting things done without a spike in blood pressure is useful only if your completed actions serve the purpose of great design. Otherwise, these personality traits, these behaviors, are entirely meaningless. They may make you friends, but they won't make you great at your job.

To be reasonable is to get along. It is to go with what is, and not what should be. It is to be satisfied, and not to strive. It is to manage, and not to lead.

This is not how businesses get built. This is not how professions improve. This is not how industries get disrupted. This is not how the world changes.

The important part of Shaw's quote is the third sentence. It's the part where the argument is formed, where the meaning of the two preceding sentences comes together to teach a lesson.

Therefore all progress depends on the unreasonable man.

For change to occur, one must be *un*reasonable. One must see the world as it should be, in its best form, at its most visionary, with its best outcomes, and then act unreasonably to achieve that standard.

This is not to grant you license to dig in your heels and take a stubborn stance on any whim or false belief you happen to possess because you believe it's right. That's not progress. The notion of being unreasonable is not about stubbornness. It's about being stubborn enough to take every step you can to achieve the quality of work you are after.

It means doing research to dissuade yourself of your own biases. It means asking more questions, listening to more answers, to find the truths you missed the first time around. It means being willing to throw out your work and start over because you're sure it can be better.

This is how the UX profession came to exist in the first place. This is how the *Internet* came to exist. Someone decided there was a better way, and pursued it, and figured out what it was, and came out the other side.

It's how all the best web businesses have been formed and grown. It's why technology has made such leaps in the past couple of decades. It's why the design of that technology has improved so much in such a short time.

The web has been built on the backs of unreasonable people. The design of technology, driven by unreasonable people, has been responsible for the mass adoption that has created the funding for the advancement of technology. Without the unreasonable people, there is no Computers section in the bookstore. There is no UX profession. There is no raised bar for the field of design.

Like it or not, if you are a designer, your job is to be one of the unreasonable people. You are a designer. This is your special power. Use it. You can be calm and deliberate and pleasant while doing it—in fact, that may help you quite a bit—but to make change, the unreasonable part of you needs to keep burning behind it all. Without you and those around you pushing and shaping and reimagining the world according to your extraordinary standards, there is no improvement.

If something is terrible, call it out. If something has a flaw, point at it (and then propose an improvement, because complaints alone are useless and annoying). If something doesn't exist that should, say why, and if it's important enough, go after it with all your might. If you're the only person who cares and you don't care enough to make it happen, then it will not happen.

Progress is made when people push hard for it. They stand for things. They forge good arguments. They convince, they challenge, they prove. It's how the seatbelt was invented. It's how America won its independence. It's how "user experience" became a common notion and a ubiquitous demand. (Fifteen years ago, a lot fewer of us were fighting this fight. It was hard then. But it was a worthy war.)

Don't be reasonable. Be successful in achieving the great outcome.

A Hard Road to Travel On

One warning:

It might be lonely. Absolutely no one becomes Steve Jobs without deep conviction and a demanding vision for the world, and no one realizes that kind of vision without alienating a few people in the process.

Making the argument when no one wants to hear it is a hard road to travel on. Calling for more research when everyone thinks their assumptions are correct can make for a lonely day.

Do it anyway. It is worth doing.

If you are someone who wants to do great work, someone who wants to craft designs that have positive effects on the people who use them—designs that make people's lives easier, and better, and more manageable—it is worth doing.

▶ The Advantage of High Standards

One of the biggest obstacles to good work is low standards. High standards help you get past the other obstacles, like people and politics (more on this in a minute). Namely, they help drive you to become a better designer. They also help drive you to the people who can help get you into better situations and projects.

About Those Elusive High Standards

In a web design context, high standards can mean great graphic design work, emotive copywriting, compelling services at approachable prices that convert well—all kinds of things. In rare cases, it can mean all of those things at once. Merely looking around at websites, it may be difficult to tell who's doing well and who's not. The trick is to compare what you think is good to what other people think is good and see how they line up. This can happen through conversations on discussion lists, news articles highlighting a company's success, journalistic reviews of up-and-coming startups, Twitter buzz, or any other method you can find to read someone's argument for why something is good or bad. The more you find and compare, the more you learn what other people think reflects quality and how their definitions compare to your own. Over time, your view of quality will change. It will become more in line with what *most* people think is good. Once you achieve that, you can spot great work from a mile away. After a few years, your high level of taste becomes second nature. Study the well-known designers. Review their work. Listen to what they say, look at what they look at. Your standards will shoot up quickly.

Now on to how high standards help you.

I want to return for a moment to what Harry Max said about moving from Unconscious Incompetence to Mastery. It happens in stages. It happens slowly. Malcolm Gladwell says it takes 10,000 hours. I said earlier it takes more than hours; it takes *feverish* hours. You can't get there without fire.

Mastery requires one other element: a devotion to the highest standard possible.

When you set your bar too low, it's too easy to design something that reaches it. When you have run-of-the-mill taste, it's too easy to design something well enough to perpetuate it. Poor design is relatively easy to achieve. Yes, you still have to have some skill, but it can be at a less-than-mediocre level. The people who design sub-par websites mostly think they are doing pretty well despite the evidence stacked against them.

UX isn't easy. It's complicated, and sophisticated, and nuanced, and time-consuming. If at any point you think this career is easy, then either you're really talented and experienced or you're not reaching far enough. You've set your bar too low, and you're reaching it handily. And that's as far as you'll ever go.

The advantage of high standards is that you will be more driven to learn the difference between an effective design and an ineffective design. You'll bother to learn what everyone means when they refer to "clean" design. You'll become adept at spotting the qualities of a good site or app and how they compare to the qualities of the sites and apps you forget about after 10 minutes and never use again. You'll pay more attention to how designs you encounter in everyday life affect you, and what made them affect you in the way they did. You'll learn why the measurability of design is so crucial (hint: because it takes your taste out of the equation and focuses your energy on whether or not the design does its job well).

High standards will drive you to do and learn more than other people.

High Standards Lead to Prowess

They say knowing is half the battle. But learning the difference between good and bad design is no small feat. In this case, knowing is not half the battle. It's more like 20 percent of the battle. A devotion to high standards doesn't automatically earn you a spot on the list of people who do good work.

A momentary digression to explain why.

I mentioned earlier that Ernest Hemingway wrote at a 4th-grade level. He used sparse, plain language, and he stuck to it throughout every piece of literature he created. But despite all those who have praised his style and success, few writers have emulated it very well.

This is because it takes years and years to learn how to write with such simplicity and appeal. You'd think it would be easier to learn to walk than to run marathons, but few people ever learn to write as simply as Hemingway did. Mostly, they write with much more complexity. In school, they teach you about complex sentences. In college, they teach you about academic writing. This is where most people leave off. They end their writing education with lessons on the most complicated and ornate writing they have ever done and will ever do. To push past it and learn once again to write at a 4th-grade level takes an obscene amount of work.

Your devotion to high standards is a powerful force. It will push you past the typical lessons and drive you to relearn the meaning of clarity and simplicity. But be prepared for this to take a long time. Knowing what's good is not the same as creating it. It took Hemingway a good long time to become Hemingway.

Moving from Unconscious Incompetence to Mastery doesn't just take years, and it doesn't just take *feverish* years. It takes an undying desire to understand quality. To study it. To strive for it. To make it your goal.

This is actually a key reason people get more humble as they get closer to Mastery. The better you are, the more aware you are of how much better you could be.

High Standards Make You More Persuasive

Over time, high standards will force you to become better at all your design skills, including your power to persuade. You'll master it out of necessity. Politics can bury you on any project, and politics can come in so many forms, you don't always even know which direction they're coming from. The difficulty can be a stakeholder trying to "manage up" to his boss. It can be a boss whose whims are more important to her than good, well-researched design decisions. It can be a designer trying to maneuver onto another project by getting more of his or her own work into the current one, even if it's built on bad ideas.

Sticking to your guns—committing to high standards—means you'll find ways to work with the situation. You'll commit to asking more questions, doing more research, showing more evidence, all in the interest of proving without a doubt that good design has to win out. That it will make them all more money. That it will help you all get closer to the *next* goal, whatever that may be.

High Standards Lead to People

In the beginning of a design career, your biggest wish is to work with people you can learn from. People who are way better than you are, way more experienced, and who can help you move quickly from novice to not-so-novice.

A devotion to high standards gets you to those people. Even if the people you're working with right now are mediocre and stifled and bored, your high standards will compel you to do all kinds of things they won't do.

Like email a professional you admire. Someone who wrote a good article or book and whom you'd like to learn more from.

In the past decade, the vast majority of my client projects have been initiated by people who had read something I'd written or who saw me speak at a conference. Besides that, I often get email from people who have read something of mine and have a follow-up question. I can safely say it is common practice for the people who care about design to reach out to other people who care about design. (Never be afraid to do it, by the way. Authors love hearing from their readers.)

A devotion to high standards will also drive you to find the best people in your company. To pick their brains. To volunteer to work with them on a project. (I've contracted several junior designers over the years after they've emailed me to ask if I'd consider hiring them for something. I know of some agencies that have done the same thing.)

It will drive the people around you to ask for your opinion more frequently. It will drive those above you to bring you into their projects.

In other words, your devotion to high standards will pull you toward other people with high standards, and attract people with high standards to you.

In short order, you'll have a pool of influential people around you. And there's no better way to learn than to learn from the best.

In the beginning of my career, I was alone on a raft somewhere out in the Pacific. I didn't know a single person who did web design. I certainly didn't think I'd ever work for one of the big companies where people did this work professionally. And even after my first web design job, it was a while before I started to meet anyone else who cared about this subject that I'd devoted so much time to.

I founded a users' group. I joined a discussion list. I emailed an author whose book I'd read. Slowly, my devotion to high standards put me in touch with all kinds of other people who felt the same way. They were designers at big companies. They were authors. Eventually, they were conference speakers. One person led to the next. Then I found myself writing a book. Then a second one. Then I was on a stage at the SxSW (South by Southwest) conference in Austin, Texas, sitting next to Christina Wodtke and in front of an audience of 700 people and getting my name out into the world. All because I was interested in defining and improving the way UX people do their work.

A devotion to high standards will take you a long way if you hold on to it.

High standards will move you from Unconscious Bad Taste to Conscious Great Taste And The Ability To Produce It. It will move you from minor projects to major ones. It will move you from a position of staying out of the way to one of leading the way.

If you don't have this devotion, get out now. You'll just exhaust yourself. Web design is tough enough to do well when you *have* the fire. Without it, you'll burn out fast.

Embrace the highest standard you can imagine and aim for it. If you do, your career could be wilder than you ever expected.

▶ Designing for Greatness

A final word on the goal of all these soft skills.

About a decade ago, I was involved in a project that involved several hundred hours of usability tests broken out over several different types of interfaces that were trendy at the time. At times, it felt a bit like one of those old torture scenes in a movie, where the protagonist is strapped to a chair with his eyes taped open and exposed to hours and hours of terrifying images flashed across the screen in front of him in bits and pieces until he loses his mind.

It felt like that for a few weeks, actually.

But then something clicked, and a sentence came to mind I've repeated many times since.

You get what you design for.

If you design an interface with infinite scrolling, you get people who will scroll infinitely. People who lose the ability to reach the end of a page. People who mash their fingers into the arrow key on the keyboard over and over. Switch to using the mouse so they can try to drag the scrollbar itself as far as it will go. Get frustrated. Give up. (This was true at the time anyway. Infinite scrolling is much more common now, so new testing is in order.)

When you put three input fields on a page—one for searching the site, one for subscribing to a newsletter, one for signing in—you get users who put whatever they have in mind into any field they happen to think might do the trick. Three fields mean three ways to do any one of these things. *Right?*

When you write a heading that says one thing, you get people who think it means something else.

This *can* be a good thing. It *can* mean you've inadvertently enabled your users to do something cool and interesting you'd never imagined and that you can now modify your product to support it because they're on to something. Twitter's hashtag support, for example. It started as a grassroots method of creating searchable topics.

Most of the time, design that leaves too much open to interpretation is a problem. Most of the time, it means you've designed something that will lose you money. And drive potential customers away. And result in all kinds of customer support email you don't understand, because you can't imagine how someone could've gotten your interface so wrong, let alone how to fix it.

You see this a few times, and you want to blame the users. It's a fluke, you think. You got it right, you're just dealing with one of those stupid users everyone talks about.

You see it a few more times, you start to think there may be something to it. *Why are so many people misinterpreting my design?*

You see it a lot, and there's no refuting it. They all see something in your design you do not. They're all doing something with your design you didn't know could be done. You intended something that isn't translating. They're not picking up what you're putting down. You used a misleading word, a misplaced text field, a strange explanation, a bit of instructions no one is noticing.

Watching a few hundred people misinterpret what you considered to be intuitive and predictable interfaces, well, that'll change you. During that months-long series of usability tests, I took great comfort in knowing that the designs being tested were not my own. And I've never been able to look at a webpage the same way. When I am assessing one, I can see the wide variety of ways a heading or a button or an interactive element could be misinterpreted. When I am designing one, I can let it rest overnight and come back to it the next day with fresh eyes and wonder *what on Earth I was thinking* and try to correct it. I can see it like a user sees it. Someone who doesn't know what it means, or what the designer meant, and who can see only what's on the screen.

I implore you to reach this point. Study enough. Watch enough. Listen enough. Do all these things so much that your brain folds in half and you see a screen as a non-designer sees it. You can't go back to the first time you saw a screen and wondered what it meant. Too late for that. You can only watch enough other people do it to internalize the feelings they have, the mysteries they're trying to unfold, the open-to-interpretation interfaces they're encountering day after day, minute after minute.

Honestly, it's amazing people can use the web at all. For all the progress we've made in improving the design of technology, most of it is still dreadfully complicated and hard to learn. It's a testament to humanity that so many people are able to overcome the craziness of our incoherent and inconsistent design work, especially from one app or site to the next, and force themselves into a working knowledge.

To *satisfice*.

It's no wonder most people use only a *few* core destination sites and apps each day. Each one has a learning curve. You stick to the ones you like. The ones you've learned. The ones you *know*.

If you can study enough, watch enough, listen enough, you can see what most people are actually dealing with day to day, and then you can apply your design knowledge to it to make it better. Instead of designing for options, you can design for defaults. Instead of designing for interpretation, you can design for specificity. Instead of designing for possibilities, you can design for clear pathways.

Then you can apply the lesson of *getting what you design for* to your own life. To your work relationships. To your goals.

Be an unreasonable designer.

Instead of designing to keep your job, design to build your career.

Instead of designing to generalize, design to be a specialist.

Instead of designing to let stakeholders lead you, design to lead them.

Instead of designing to be as good as always, design to be better than ever.

Instead of designing to measure your life in successes and failures, design to do what makes you proud, in a way that makes you proud.

Do it through strong ethics. With a strong will. With steadfast beliefs. With high standards.

Extremely high standards.

You can design your role. Your skill set. Your communication. How people react to you. How you react to situations, to people, to constraints, to changes.

You get what you design for.

Design to lead.

▶ Index

A

answers
    finding to design questions, 72–75
    restating, 129
argument, 120–138. *See also*
        communication
    asking questions in, 91–93, 95–97,
        125–127
    educating clients via, 129–130
    presenting, 102, 105, 121–122,
        131–135
    supporting ideas in, 131–135,
        136–138
    teaching team members skills of,
        160–162
asking questions
    about own work, 91–93
    benefits of, 95–97
    as designers, 126–127
    listening and, 125–127
assumptions, 137

B

backing up design ideas, 131–138
Blink (Gladwell), 128, 170

C

calmness
    effectiveness and, 190, 192
    gaining respect via, 141–143
    ignoring distractions, 143–145

clarity
    communication and design,
        115, 117
    enabling comprehension with,
        114–115
    in thinking, 104–105
clients
    communication breakdowns with,
        100–101
    convincing, 121–122
    coordinating with in-house
        design teams, 166–167
    educating, 115–117, 129–130, 161
    explaining changes to, 131–135
    mapping messages to, 108–111
    understanding dynamics with
        corporate, 85–91
code-hoarders, 159
collaborative process, 150–152
communication, 100–117. *See also*
        spoken communications;
        written communications
    asking questions, 91–93, 95–97,
        125–127
    breakdowns in, 66–67, 100–101
    clarity in, 101–105, 115, 117
    communicating design
        psychology, 76–78
    design as communication,
        101–102
    educating clients on design,
        115–117, 129–130, 161
    enabling comprehension of,
        114–115